T0128178

MARRIAGE
101

A PRACTICAL GUIDE TO ENJOYING
MARRIAGE AS GOD DESIGNED

GREG MEISEL

WESTBOW
PRESS®
A DIVISION OF THOMAS NELSON
& ZONDERVAN

WestBow Press books may be ordered through booksellers or by contacting:

WestBow Press
A Division of Thomas Nelson & Zondervan
1663 Liberty Drive
Bloomington, IN 47403
www.westbowpress.com
1 (866) 928-1240

ISBN: 978-1-9736-4509-2 (sc)
ISBN: 978-1-9736-4511-5 (hc)
ISBN: 978-1-9736-4510-8 (e)

Library of Congress Control Number: 2018913367

Print information available on the last page.

WestBow Press rev. date: 11/15/2018

Contents

Dedication

I want to dedicate this book to my Lord and Savior Jesus Christ. Without His wonderful work in my heart and life none of this would be possible. My humble efforts at writing and counseling are only because He chooses to work through me for His glory. May He always be glorified through every part of my life and someday my death (Phil. 1:20-21). I pray the He ministers to you and encourages you as you read and work through this book.

I also want to dedicate this book to every person that cares enough about his or her marriage relationship to want to improve it. A decade ago when my wife Wendy and I first heard about Caring for the Heart counseling, we already had a good marriage. However, we cared enough about our relationship to want an even closer and more connected relationship. We have never regretted that decision. We had no idea then that because we resolved our own issues and built a closer marriage, we would be able to help many other couples grow in their respective marriages. This book is dedicated to every reader. Maybe you already have a good marriage. It can be even better! Maybe you are experiencing struggles in your marriage. This book can help you to resolve those struggles. I want to thank you for caring enough about your marriage relationship to purchase and complete this book. An adventure lies ahead of you. Some parts of this book may not be easy to work through, but they are important. An adventure always forces us out of our comfort zones. So get ready.

The adventure begins!

Foreword

The Bible clearly describes the importance of understanding God's design for marriage. God desires that each married couple experience the joy and fulfillment of life with their spouse. Being emotionally connected in relationship to each other is essential if a couple is to fulfill God's design for them.

In his book, Marriage 101, Greg Meisel shares many of his personal times of connecting to his wife and the opportunities he has had to understand and care about her heart. Greg weaves together his own personal journey with the Biblical directives a couple can use to experience the oneness God designed for a couple.

The Bible shares specific ways a husband and wife can connect to honor Christ and reflect His relationship with His Bride, the church. Greg identifies these Biblical principles in the chapters of this book to encourage you to become Christ-like in your relationship and responses to your spouse. I would encourage you to apply to your marriage relationship the concepts that are introduced in Marriage 101. If you incorporate them in your marriage, you will become emotionally connected to each other and experience the fulfillment and excitement that God designed for couples.

I trust you will enjoy reading Greg's book and that you will take the time to complete the chapter assignments. Your heart will be encouraged, as mine is, to know the fulfillment God designed for your own marriage. I encourage you to share the Biblical principles with others, so they can experience emotional connection with their spouse.

John Regier, Director
Caring for the Heart Ministries

Acknowledgements

I want to thank my wonderful wife Wendy for all her support and encouragement. This book has been a labor of love than has taken several years because of our busy counseling schedule. If it was not for her continual encouragement, I probably would have given up a long time ago. She challenged me to schedule blocks of time to write, which allowed me to complete this book. Wendy, thank you for always being there for me and supporting me in everything I have attempted. I love counseling alongside you, but most of all I love our relationship. To answer the question King Solomon poses in Proverbs 31:10, "I have found a virtuous wife and, yes, her worth is far above rubies."

I also want to thank both of my grown "kids". My son Jared and daughter Melanie, along with their respective families, are a huge blessing and a great encouragement. I especially want to thank Melanie for all the hours she spent proofreading this book. Thanks for all your help, Mel.

Many of the charts, prayers and concepts used in Section Two: Practical Projects for Marriage were based on concepts originated by John Regier of *Caring for the Heart Ministries*, Colorado Springs, CO. This book would not have been possible without the help and counsel of John Regier. A number of years ago now, John counseled Wendy and I. He led us to Jesus to heal our hearts. Our lives and marriage relationship have not been the same. John has always been there to encourage and mentor as we opened our own counseling ministry *Caring for the Heart – New England*. John, thank you for all the hours you invested in us. Only when you get to heaven will you know all the people you have impacted through your service for the Lord.

I also wish to thank John's wife, Barb Regier. Barb likes to stay behind the scenes; however, she has always been a great encouragement to Wendy and I. Barb, thank you for the times you welcomed us into your home, as well as the many other times we have spent together at various conferences across the country. Barb, we are blessed every time we are with you.

Thank you also to the board of directors at *Caring for the Heart – New England*. Wendy and I appreciate all the time you invest and your support for this ministry. I especially appreciate that you allowed me to take time from counseling to finish this book.

Welcome to Marriage 101

A young couple was visiting with an older couple celebrating their 50th wedding anniversary. "Fifty years!" the young husband exclaimed, "That is a long time to be married to one person." The old gentleman looked over at his wife with love in his eyes and said, "It would have been a lot longer without her."

Welcome! Whether you are engaged anticipating a lifetime together, are newly married or are marriage veterans wedded for years; I want to welcome you to this study. No matter what our level of experience or inexperience, for that matter, each of us can grow in our marriage relationship. When I married my precious wife over thirty years ago, I thought I understood everything there was to know about marriage. I had read several books on Christian marriage and I was sure I knew everything I needed to know in order for Wendy and I to have a perfect marriage. Before the first year of marriage was over, I began to understand how little I really knew about marriage in general and about my bride in particular. Now with more than 30 years behind us, I realize that there is still a lot about marriage that I don't know. Wendy and I enjoy a wonderfully close, emotionally-connected relationship; but we know we still have room for improvement. We are so committed to each other and to our relationship that we have determined to keep building and strengthening our relationship until God takes one of us home.

I would encourage you to make a life-long decision to continually improve your marriage relationship. Never allow your marriage to become static. The Bible has quite a bit to say about the importance of the believer growing rather than stagnating in his relationship with the Lord. (Rom. 12:1-2; 1 Cor. 9:24-27; Phil. 3:12-14; Rev. 3:15-19) Each of us also needs to continue growing in our relationship with the one person on earth who should be most important to us – our spouse. We can each improve in our ability to understand and appreciate our respective spouses. Men can grow in their ability to sacrificially love and care for their wives. Wives can improve in their ability to love and respect their husbands. Complacency has no place in the Christian life or the marriage relationship.

My prayer is that as you go through this book you will grow closer to your mate and your Heavenly Father. Along with learning new information and principles, you will have practical opportunities to apply what you learn. My goal is for each couple who goes through this study to learn to understand and enjoy marriage as God designed.

Welcome to the adventure that I call Marriage 101.

Called to Care
Greg Meisel
Caring for the Heart – New England

Aim: The purpose of this book is to help each couple gain a biblical understanding of marriage and develop emotional intimacy in their relationship. Each couple will learn how to meet each other's deepest needs and connect on a heart level.

What makes Marriage 101 different? There are many great marriage books and courses available. Any Christian book store will probably have an entire section dedicated to the plethora of marriage books and courses available. So why am I adding one more resource to a market already flooded with marriage helps? Marriage 101 comes out of our own personal struggles as well hundreds of hours spent counseling other couples. As we counseled Christian couples, we found that many of them have read many of the books. They know a lot of the principles taught in marriage books and courses; however, what they know is making no difference at all in their relationships. In our counseling we use some fairly simple principles to help couples learn how to connect emotionally and respond to each other in Christ-like ways. I wrote this book in order to teach some of those same principles to more couples. The first part of this book will help you understand marriage as God designed it. The second section of Marriage 101 includes a lot of activities and practical applications to help each couple build an emotionally-connected marriage relationship. Individual couples can work through this book together or it can be done by couples in a small group setting. For these reasons, Marriage 101 is different than any other marriage helps of which I am aware. The object of this course is not just to teach you more about marriage; it is to help you develop the connected, fulfilling relationship that God intends for you and your spouse.

> For I know the thoughts that I think toward you, says the LORD, thoughts of peace and not of evil, to give you a future and a hope. (Jer. 29:11 NKJV)

> All Scripture verses are from the New King James Version, except where noted otherwise.

- God has good things planned for us. Let's begin the journey…

[For Couples]
Look in your spouse's eyes and ask each other these questions:

1. Do you remember the first time we met?
2. What did you think of me that first time we met?
3. What first attracted you to me?
4. Why did you decide to marry me?
5. What was your favorite part of our engagement?
6. What was your favorite part of our honeymoon?
7. What have you enjoyed the most about our marriage?
8. How would you like our marriage to benefit from this study?
9. What would you like our marriage to be like ten years from now?

• Go to the Prayer Time on the next page.

[For Small Groups]
Let's get to know each other:

1. Please introduce yourself to the group. What is your name?
2. How long have you been married? (If engaged, when will you be married?)
3. Do you have any children? If so, what are their ages?
4. What attracted you to your spouse before you were married?
5. Tell us about the proposal. Who proposed to whom? Where? When? How?
6. How long was your engagement period before your wedding?
7. What has been the best part of your marriage? (If engaged, what is the best part of your relationship?)
8. What is your favorite memory from your time together?
9. What has been one of the struggles in your marriage? (If engaged, what is one of the struggles in your relationship?)
10. What do you want to get out of this study?

Prayer Time: (Each chapter closes with a prayer time. The picture of Jesus with the girl marking each prayer time was drawn by a teen girl with whom Wendy worked. She drew this picture of what Jesus showed her when she prayed and gave Him all her pain. The picture is a reminder that Jesus loves to care for us when we come to Him in prayer. We can pour out our hearts to Him.)

Theme Thought: God has good plans for your marriage relationship.

- Thank God that He does have good things planned for you, your spouse and your relationship
- Thank God for the opportunity to spend the next 12 weeks focusing on your marriage relationship.
- Ask God to strengthen and improve your relationship during the next 12 weeks.
- Confess any way that you have doubted God's good plans for your marriage.
- Confess any way you way blamed God for the struggles in your marriage.
- Ask God to give you increased hope and enthusiasm for your future marriage relationship.

Closing Prayer:
Jesus, I want to thank You that You care about my spouse and me. Thank You that You care about our relationship. You

know that we struggle sometimes in our relationship. I know that You care about that. I know that You have good things planned for us and our relationship. Jesus, can You show me what you want my relationship with my spouse to be like?

PAUSE. Allow Jesus to speak to your heart.

Thank You, Jesus. Amen.

Section One

The Biblical Basis for Marriage

1

GOD'S PURPOSE IN MARRIAGE

Any study of marriage must begin with God. For, like all creation, marriage begins with God. Marriage was God's idea. He designed marriage. He created marriage. We know that everything God created was *very good* (Genesis 1:31), meaning it was extremely beautiful, pleasant or agreeable, and that includes marriage. What was God's purpose for marriage? What did God intend for the marriage relationship to be? To fully understand marriage, we need to find the answers to those questions. We find those answers in God's Word.

Read Genesis 1:26-27, 2:15-25.

The woman was the only part of creation formed out of another living being. The animals were formed from the dust of the ground. Man was formed from the dust of the ground, but not woman. She was formed from man. The man and the woman did not just share a common Creator or a common origin, like the animals did. They actually shared a common identity.

1. Why do you think God created the man first before the woman?

   _____

   _____

   _____

_____

_____

_____

_____

_____

_____

2. Which did God give man first, a vocation or a marriage relationship? (v. 15)

_____

_____

3. Was Adam's vocation completely satisfying? (v. 18-20)

_____

_____

_____

_____

4. Why do you think God did things in this order?

_____

_____

_____

_____

And the LORD God said, "*It is* **not good** that man should be alone; I will make him a **helper comparable** to him." (Gen. 2:18 NKJV; boldface added)

Then the LORD God said, "It is *not good* for the man to be alone; I will make him a *helper suitable* for him." (Gen. 2:18 NASB; italics added)

Good actually means it is not best for man to be alone. God had a better plan than for man to live life alone. Alone has the sense of a separation or being only part of a whole. It seems that God created man as part of a whole with a natural desire and need to be completed by another. God did not design man to be self-sufficient or self-sustaining. God designed and created Adam with an innate need for someone to complement and complete him before Eve was created. Before Eve existed, Adam needed her.

5. Why did God say, "It is not good that man should be alone"?

_____

_____

_____

_____

_____

_____

God intervened in Adam's situation to remedy his incompleteness. God said, "I will make a helper comparable to him" (NKJV) or "a helper suitable for him" (NASB). The Hebrew word translated helper literally means help. It is the same word used in Psalms in reference to Jehovah (Yahweh) our

Help. (Pss. 33:20, 70:5, 115:9-11) The word translated comparable or suitable literally means the part opposite or counterpart. In other words, the woman was made as the perfect complement to the man. She was intentionally made different from the man, but she was made to complete the man. By complementing and completing the man, the woman was able to help him. Eve satisfied the innate need for companionship and completion, with which Adam was created. Eve did not just complete and complement Adam physically; but she did so in every sense. She also fulfilled her husband spiritually, emotionally, and mentally.

6. How do you think Eve demonstrated in their relationship that she was a helper suitable for Adam?

_____

_____

_____

_____

_____

_____

God created man and all the animals from the ground (vv. 7, 19); however, woman was created differently. She was made from Adam's body – his rib. (vv. 21, 22). The woman was the only living being created out of another living being. God made two unique individuals out of one being. This graphically demonstrates the closeness and intimacy of a married couple. Every time Adam looked at his wife, he saw part of himself. In God's eyes a married couple shares one unique identity. (Matt. 19:4-6; Mark 10:6-9) He no longer views them as two separate individuals. God views them as two essential parts of one whole or two unique beings bonded together in one special relationship.

7. What does it mean to you personally that God created woman differently than every other created being? Husband, what does this mean about the way you treat your wife? Wife, how does this affect your self-image and how you see you relationship with your husband?

_____

_____

_____

_____

_____

_____

_____

_____

_____

And the LORD God caused a deep sleep to fall on Adam, and he slept; and He took one of his ribs, and closed up the flesh in its place.

Then the rib which the LORD God had taken from man He made into a woman, and He brought her to the man.

And Adam said: "This *is* now bone of my bones And flesh of my flesh; She shall be called Woman, Because she was taken out of Man." (Gen. 2:21-23)

From the creation of the marriage relationship it was to be an extremely close connected relationship. Marriage was to be a mutually fulfilling, beneficial relationship. God created marriage as a relationship where each spouse complements and completes the other in every possible way. Eve enabled Adam to better fulfill his day-to-day responsibilities (Gen. 2:18-20). Adam and Eve were able to enjoy a close, connected relationship, which was impossible outside of marriage (vv. 23-25). From the beginning, Adam was responsible to be the spiritual leader in the relationship, and Eve followed his leadership (2:16-17, 3:2-3). Adam enjoyed telling Eve what God had told him, and she believed him. She naturally followed his leadership.

8. What do you think God intended for the relationship between husband and wife when He created marriage.

_____

_____

_____

_____

_____

_____

_____

_____

_____

Adam and Eve's pre-fall marriage relationship was closer than any relationship since sin entered the world. They were able to join their hearts by freely communicating, sharing, and caring. They were able to join their souls in walking with and worshipping their Creator. They were able to join their bodies in the perfect sexual experience where they could give themselves freely to meet the needs of their spouse. Negative thoughts and emotions did not yet exist, so Adam and Eve were able to fully enjoy spiritual, emotional, intellectual, and physical connection in their marriage relationship. This is what God intended for marriage. God intended for marriage to be the one relationship where a person can experience unconditional love and acceptance by another person. It was to be the one relationship where a person could give himself totally to meet the needs of his spouse and experience fulfillment in the process. It was to be the one relationship where two people live life together in a dynamic partnership and union, which enables them to be more creative, productive, and effective than if they lived their lives alone.

> Therefore a man shall *leave* his father and mother and be *joined* to his wife, and they shall become one flesh. (Gen. 2:24; italics added)

The Hebrew word translated as leave means literally to loosen or by implication to relinquish or forsake. It is the same word God uses throughout the Old Testament to describe how Israel had forsaken Him. It describes the breaking of a connection or relationship. When a person gets married the relationship that person has with his or her parents is no longer the primary relationship in his or her life. Although we are always to honor or value our parents (Exod. 20:12; Eph. 6:2-3); when we marry, we are joined to our spouse. The word translated as joined actually means adhered to. A man and woman are joined together or adhesively bonded to each other in a marriage. Marriage is the intricate, integral adhesion of two incomplete persons into one complete, connected whole. The marriage relationship is to be our most important human relationship. Our relationship with our spouse supersedes and eclipses all other earthly relationships. Only our relationship with God is more important than our marriage relationship. A close relationship with God will never damage our marriage relationship. Actually, the opposite is true. The marriage relationship is unique, in that, the closer we grow to our heavenly Father, the closer we will grow toward our spouse. I often use the illustration of a triangle to illustrate marriage. God is at the apex (top) and the spouses are at each of the bottom corners. As each spouse moves closer to God, he or she will also grow closer to his or her spouse.

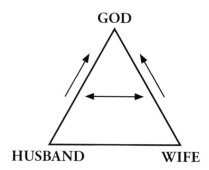

9. It was God's plan for a man to leave his father and mother and be joined to his wife (Gen. 2:24). In what ways did you leave your father and mother after you were married? How well did you join to your spouse? Did you find the joining to your spouse easy or difficult? Which parts came easiest? Which were the hardest?

_____

_____

_____

_____

_____

_____

_____

_____

_____

And they were both naked, the man and his wife, and
were not ashamed. (Gen. 2:25)

Adam and Eve were naked emotionally, intellectually, spiritually
and physically, yet they were without any negative emotions or thoughts
accompanying their nakedness. They were totally open, honest and
transparent with each other. They were able to freely bare their souls,
hearts, minds and bodies to each other without any shame or fear. They
had no fear of rejection. Neither worried that he or she would fail to
meet the other's expectations. They had no secrets from each other. They
had no walls in their relationship. There was nothing about which they
could not talk freely and openly. Adam and Eve, in this pre-fall existence,
experienced the perfect transparency, intimacy and oneness that God
intended to be an essential and central component of every marriage.

10. Why do you think God included verse 25 in this original marriage
    passage? What does it tell us about the marriage relationship?
    What can this short verse teach us about the marriage relationship?

_____

_____

_____

_____

_____

_____

Marriage: The Perfect Symbiotic Relationship

In biology symbiosis is the term used to describe two dissimilar organisms living together. There are different types of symbiotic relationships. In one form of symbiosis is *parasitism* where one organism (the parasite) derives food and/or shelter from the other (the host). In this type of relationship, one organism is benefited but the other is damaged and may even be killed as a result of the relationship. Another form of symbiosis is *commensalism,* where one organism is helped but the other is neither helped nor injured. The third form of symbiosis is *mutualism,* a relationship where both organism benefit.

Marriage is a symbiotic relationship. God designed it that way. God designed marriage as a relationship where two dissimilar, incomplete people unite together in a God-honoring whole. In the marriage relationship as God designed it, both spouses benefit from the marriage relationship. Marriage was to be the perfect symbiotic or mutualistic relationship. Marriage was meant to make us stronger, better, and more mature.

God designed marriage to be a very good thing. However, something cataclysmic happened. The marriage relationship was dramatically and detrimentally impacted. Instead of the mutually-beneficial relationship God designed, many marriages have become commensalistic or even parasitic relationships. Each spouse may struggle to control the other in order to get what he or she needs from the relationship. One spouse may damage the other with verbal, physical, spiritual, or even sexual abuse. One spouse may disconnect from the other and seek to get his or her needs met outside the marriage relationship. What God designed as the most special human relationship has been warped and twisted. The relationship where each of us was to feel safe, secure, and accepted; instead became a source of tremendous pain and rejection. What could cause such devastating damage to God's wonderful gift of marriage? We will look at that in more detail in the next chapter.

Review:

Use your sanctified imagination to answer these questions.

1. What do you think Adam thought when God brought Eve to him?

   _____

   _____

   _____

   _____

2. What do you think Eve thought when God brought her to Adam?

   _____

   _____

   _____

   _____

3. What do you think Adam and Eve talked about when they met? Who initiated the conversation?

   _____

   _____

   _____

   _____

More seriously…

> In this lesson, we saw that marriage was to be the one relationship where two people live life together in a dynamic partnership and union, which enables them to be more creative, productive, and effective than if they lived their lives alone.

4. Do you believe this? Why or why not?

_____

_____

_____

_____

5. Have you experienced this is your marriage? Why or why not?

_____

_____

_____

_____

The author made the following statement:
Only our relationship with God is more important than our marriage relationship. A close relationship with God will never damage our marriage relationship. Actually, the opposite is true. The marriage relationship is unique, in that, the closer we grow to our heavenly Father, the closer we will grow toward our spouse.

6. Do you agree with this? Why or why not?

_____

_____

_____

_____

7. Does your relationship with God affect your marriage? How?

_____

_____

_____

_____

8. What is one thing you have learned from this lesson which you can apply to your marriage relationship?

_____

_____

_____

_____

Prayer Time:

Theme Thought: Your spouse is God's special gift to you.

- Thank God for the spouse He has given you.
- Ask God to give you a greater appreciation for your spouse this week.
- Confess any way that you have not appreciated your spouse in the past week.
- Ask God to show you how you can express appreciation to your spouse this week.

Closing Prayer:
Jesus, I want to thank You for my spouse. (Spouse's name) is really a special gift from You. I admit that sometimes I take (spouse's name) for granted. Sometimes I think negative thoughts about him (or her). Jesus, I confess that sin to You and ask You to forgive me. Will You help me to see his (or her) good characteristics? (Spouse's name) is a special creation of Yours. You handcrafted him (or her). You gave Your life for him (or her). (Spouse's name) is very special to You,

isn't he (or she)? Jesus can You show me what You think of
(spouse's name)?

PAUSE, allow Jesus to speak to your heart.

Jesus, will You help me to value my spouse the way You do?

Thank You, Jesus. Amen.

2

SIN'S IMPACT ON MARRIAGE

The worst natural disaster in recorded history took place in central China during 1931. An unusually heavy snowfall during the winter caused the massive flooding of three large rivers during the spring. Also during the summer, 10 typhoons swept through the region. Nanjing City, which was the capital of China at the time, was surrounded by 100,000 square kilometers of water for weeks. The death toll due to the catastrophic flooding and subsequent outbreak of diseases is estimated between 3.7 and 4 million people. In one night alone, 200,000 drown in their sleep when the Huai River flooded the surrounding countryside. As terrible as the 1931 China floods were, today we will look at a much more catastrophic event.

We will be studying a universal tragedy, which traumatized and impacted every person ever born. This cataclysmic event also damaged every marriage relationship in the past, present, and future.

We saw in the last chapter that God created marriage as something wonderful. Marriage was designed as the marvelous spiritual, intellectual, emotional, and physical union of two incomplete individuals into a God-honoring whole. God designed and created marriage as a safe, mutually beneficial relationship.

In this chapter, we will look at how the introduction of sin into the human race impacted the marriage relationship.

In his epic poem *Paradise Lost*, John Milton contemplates mankind's fall.

> *What cause moved our Grand Parents in that happy State,*
> *Favour'd of Heav'n so highly, to fall off*
> *From their Creator, and transgress his Will*
> *For one restraint, Lords of the World besides?*
> *Who first seduc'd them to that fowl revolt?*
> *Th' infernal Serpent, he it was, whose guile*
> *Stird up with Envy and Revenge, deceiv'd*
> *The Mother of Mankind...*

Read Genesis 3:1-24.

Every good story has an element of risk. Every tale has some inherent danger. Every legend has a hero and a villain. Every western has a lawman and a desperado. Every fairy tale has a good guy and a bad guy. Every good movie has some evil that must be defeated, even if it only involves the main character overcoming issues in his or her own life. For every protagonist, there is always an antagonist. This transcendent theme of good versus evil fills our literature and our cinema because it is an essential part of life as we know it. Whether they know it or not, every person is involved in a universal conflict between good and evil.

In Genesis 1 and 2 we meet the ultimate Good Guy – our loving Creator. These introductory chapters of the greatest book ever written introduce us to the Author of this book who is the Supreme Protagonist. In Genesis 3 we are introduced to the ultimate bad guy. This enemy of the Creator and His creation is known by many names. Here he is simply called the serpent (see also 2 Cor. 11:3; Rev. 20:2). In other places he is called the Devil (Matt. 4:1; John 8:44), Satan (Job 1:6; Acts 26:18), Lucifer (Isa. 14:12), the ruler of this world (John 14:30; 16:11), the god of this age (2 Cor. 4:4), our adversary (1 Pet. 5:8), an angel of light (2 Cor. 11:14), the enemy (Matt. 13:39; Luke 10:19) and the great dragon (Rev. 12:9; 20:2). This formidable antagonist first enters the picture in this chapter.

Verse one of Genesis 3 tells us that serpent was more *cunning* or *crafty* than any other creature. The Hebrew word actually means subtle, shrewd or sly. This antagonist was an expert at subterfuge and persuasion. He hatched a plan to attack the One he despised through the Protagonist's handiwork. That was possible because God's heart was bound to mankind when He chose to love us. So Satan sought to hurt Almighty God by attacking the objects of God's love. The first step in his plan was to approach the woman. The enemy didn't come to Adam and Eve when they are together. He singled Eve out and approached her alone.

1. Why do you think Satan approached Eve alone when he wanted to tempt mankind? Why didn't he approach Adam or approach the two of them when they were together?

_____

_____

_____

_____

In Alaska and northern Canada, wolf packs will follow herds of caribou, which often number in the hundreds and even thousands. The wolves do not attack the whole herd. They study the herd from a distance, looking for sick, weak or injured members of the herd. Once they identify one weaker caribou, the wolves work together to isolate that lone caribou from the rest of the herd. As long as their chosen victim stays with the remainder of the herd it is safe, but when the wolves separate it from its companions, death is certain.

One of our enemy's primary strategies is to isolate and destroy, just like the wolf packs of the north. Satan always tries to divide married couples. He has a multitude of strategies he uses in his constant attempts to isolate spouses from each other. The enemy hates to see couples connecting emotionally, intellectually, physically and especially spiritually. He rejoices when we allow walls to develop in our relationships that prevent us from connecting. He encourages each of us to think the worst of his spouse. He wants you to believe that any problems in your marriage is your spouse's fault.

2. What practical applications to your own marriage can you draw from Satan's method of isolating and tempting Eve?

_____

_____

_____

_____

A number of years ago, my family and I spent a day at the Gettysburg Civil War Battlefield. I remember the sense of awe I felt walking the ground where so many men gave their lives for a cause in which they dearly believed. Seminary Ridge, the Peach Orchard, the Wheatfield, Bloody Angle, Devil's Den – all of these places have a different meaning for me now. The part of the battlefield that touched me the most was Little Roundtop. That rocky little hill is not much to look at. Little Roundtop is really nothing like it is portrayed in the well-known movie named after this three-day battle. As I stood on that rocky knoll, I remembered the scene from the movie when Colonel Joshua Chamberlain and his 20th Maine regiment were ordered to defend the south side of that little hill. The 20th Maine was protecting the extreme left of the Union line. They were the only ones keeping the Confederates from moving around the flank and attacking the Union line from the rear, which would have brought another dismal defeat to the Union cause and death to many Union soldiers. Colonel Chamberlain was ordered to hold his position to the last. The Maine regiment did just that. They repelled wave after wave of Confederate attackers until their ammunition was nearly depleted. The valiant colonel was determined to hold his position. So when the ammo was gone, he did the unthinkable. He ordered a bayonet charge and led his men charging down the hill into the advancing enemy troops. The Confederates were so shaken by the surprising bravery of the Maine troops that they threw down their muskets and surrendered to the charging Union soldiers. Thanks to the tenacity and determination of Colonel Chamberlain and the 20th Maine, not only was the entire battle line kept safe, but the Union won a great victory that second day of fighting at Gettysburg.

I share this true-life story for one reason. We can learn a lesson from Joshua Chamberlain. We must be just as determined that we will not give into the enemy in our respective marriage relationships. You must determine to not allow him to isolate you from your spouse. You will not allow walls to grow in your relationship. You must hold the ground of your marriage against the enemy at all times. You need to be totally committed to keeping communication open. Nothing in your life is more important than staying connected with your spouse.

3. How have you seen the enemy try to divide you and your spouse? Can you think of one time that you didn't handle it right? How should you have handled it?

_____

_____

_____

_____

> So when the woman saw that the tree *was* **good** for food, that it *was* **pleasant** to the eyes, and a tree desirable to make *one* wise, she took of its fruit and ate. She also gave to her husband with her, and he ate. (Gen. 3:6 NKJV; boldface added)

In this verse, we read Eve's response to Satan's temptation. She does respond to the serpent's carefully crafted comments by examining the fruit. She finds it good and pleasant. The Hebrew word translated *good* actually means agreeable, beautiful or beneficial and *pleasant* actually means desire or longing. The fruit looked delicious and Eve began desiring it or longing to taste it. As a result, she gives into her desires and eats the fruit. She also shares it with her husband. Adam, knowing full well that he is disobeying his Creator, also chooses to eat the fruit. Instantly, mankind fell from innocence and a perfect relationship with God into sin and depravity. This willful disobedience of the Creator sent a tsunami of titanic destruction sweeping through every facet of human existence. Mankind was separated from God. Disease, pain, and death entered creation for the first time (Rom. 5:12-19; 6:23). The enemy now ruled the world and the human race (John 8:44; 14:30; 16:11; Eph. 2:2; 1 John 5:19). From that point forward all creation would experience death, decay, and entropy. The Garden of Eden was ground zero for the most universally catastrophic event in history. The fall of mankind impacted every person, every relationship, and every creature. It affected both the physical and spiritual realms.

The main focus of this study is the effect of that fall on the marriage relationship. Adam and Eve fell as individuals; however, their sin impacted their marriage and all their relationships.

4. Have you ever wanted something very badly, which you knew was not good for you or your marriage relationship? Did you give into that temptation or not? What happened?

_____

_____

_____

_____

> Then the eyes of both of them were opened, and they knew that they *were* naked; and they sewed fig leaves together and made themselves coverings. (Gen. 3:7)

Satan was right. Did you ever think of that? Satan promised Eve that if she and her husband disobeyed God and ate the fruit, their eyes would be open so they could know good and evil (Gen. 3:5). Verse 7 says that is what happened. Their eyes were instantly opened and they now knew they were naked. The Hebrew word *know* in both these verses is *"yada"*, a word referring to intimate knowledge. It is the same word used in Gen. 4:1 to describe Adam's intimate knowledge of his wife through sexual intercourse. Pre-Fall Adam and Eve had intimate knowledge of goodness.

Post-fall they had intimate, experiential knowledge of evil. God never intended for mankind to have this kind of intimate knowledge of evil.

5. How did Adam and Eve's knowledge of good and evil change when they sinned?

    _____

    _____

    _____

    _____

    …but I want you to be wise in what is good and innocent in what is evil. (Rom. 16:19b NASB)

6. Look at Romans 16:19b. How does God want us to "know" good and evil?

    _____

    _____

    _____

    _____

God created marriage to be a wonderfully caring, transparent relationship. However, the instant this couple sinned, their marriage relationship was changed forever. They saw each other differently. The perfect innocence, transparency and acceptance they had experienced before was gone. After they sinned, Adam and Eve experienced shame, embarrassment and fear for the first time. Their first reaction was to attempt to hide from each other. The wonderful unity and openness they knew before disappeared. Now they feared rejection and failure. Now they felt the need to protect themselves. Now each thought about himself first. Now each wanted his or her own needs met first and foremost. Each worried that he would fail to meet the other's expectations. They no longer lovingly viewed each other as God's special gift; instead they looked at each other with fear and distrust. Each saw the other as someone who might hurt them. So, they hid behind fig leaves – their feeble attempt to protect themselves.

7. What do you think Adam and Eve thought and felt when "the eyes of both of them were opened"?

_____

_____

_____

_____

> And they heard the sound of the LORD God walking in the garden in the cool of the day, and Adam and his wife hid themselves from the presence of the LORD God among the trees of the garden. (Gen. 3:8)

Not only was Adam and Eve's marital relationship impacted, but even more importantly their relationship with their Creator was changed forever. It was normal for God to walk in the garden and fellowship with this couple. They were His special creation – the objects of His love. God enjoyed spending time with them, and they enjoyed fellowshipping with their Creator. When Adam and Eve heard God approaching, they would rush to be with Him. Together they were able to freely worship and fellowship with God. The three of them were able to commune in a way that they all enjoyed and found fulfilling. This communion with their Creator fulfilled Adam and Eve's deepest spiritual cravings, but that was before they disobeyed Him.

I remember as a little boy, waiting expectantly for my dad to get home from work. At the time my dad was working 8:00am to 5:00pm as a foreman in a factory. As soon as I finished my lunch, I would begin watching for him to come home. I would keep watch out our living room window, hoping to see his car approaching. When he finally pulled into the driveway, I would rush to the door to meet him. One day was very different. I was playing in the living room and broke something. I ran and hid in the kitchen pantry. I remember the fear I felt, hiding in that small, dark room. I don't know how long I hid there, but finally my dad came and found me. I must have been a pitiful sight, cowering in the dark. He swept me into his arms and told me that He loved me and it was okay.

Because of sin, mankind's relationship with God was changed forever. The instant Adam and Eve disobeyed Him, their relationship with God was broken. They no longer had a right to fellowship with Him. So, they ran and hid. Just as I hid from my dad because I knew I had done something wrong, they realized they had transgressed God's command. Now when they heard God approaching, they no longer felt joy and eager anticipation. They now felt emotions they had never experienced before.

8. What emotions do you think Adam and Eve experienced when they "heard the sound of the Lord God walking in the garden"?

_____

_____

_____

_____

9. After Adam and Eve sinned, how was their relationship with God changed?

_____

_____

_____

_____

Read Genesis 3:9-21.

Adam and Eve are hiding in the trees. God doesn't just leave them there. He pursues them. He calls them. He confronts them. He judges their sin. God cares too much about humanity in general, and these two people in particular, to just let them go. God didn't just turn His back on mankind. He doesn't annihilate them with a single word, although He could have done so. Instead God searches them out and confronts them.

10. Look at the Scripture passage given above. What are some things that happened in this passage that had never happened before? Also, what happened in Adam and Eve's relationship that had never happened before?

_____

_____

_____

_____

11. How do you see God's loving provision in this passage?

_____

_____

_____

_____

At the end of Genesis 2, Adam and Eve are enjoying a wonderful, connected, transparent relationship. At the end of Genesis 3, these same two people are fugitives, evicted from God's special place of blessing. Their lives would never be the same. Their relationship would never be the same. Making a living would now require hard work. Having a fulfilling, emotionally-connected marriage would take even more work. No matter how good our marriages may be, none of us has experienced the Edenic bliss our ancestors knew before their fall. Good marriages take work. The good news is that any of us can experience all that God wants us to have in our marriage. The bad news is that because we are sinners it takes works and it goes against our nature. Our fallen nature compels us to be self-focused in our relationship. You and I naturally want to blame our spouses for problems and difficulties in our marriages. We want to "fix" our spouses.

In the next lesson, we will be looking at God's purpose for your marriage. I want to help you have a God-blessed, emotionally-connected, love-filled marriage. Before I can teach you how to build that kind of relationship, I need to give you a warning.

 Warning:

In order to learn from this study so that you can experience the kind of relationship God wants you to have you <u>must</u> do the following.

- Focus on yourself and how you need to change to make your marriage better.
- Commit to applying the principles learned in this course to your marriage relationship.

Review:

Use your sanctified imagination to answer these questions.

1. What do you think went through Eve's mind when the serpent started talking to her?

   _____

   _____

   _____

   _____

2. What do you think Eve thought when she saw the tree was "good for food, pleasant to the eyes and desirable to make one wise"? What did Eve say when she handed her husband that forbidden fruit to eat? What do you think went through Adam's mind?

   _____

   _____

   _____

   _____

3. What do you think Adam and Eve thought when they "heard the sound of the Lord God walking in the garden"? What emotions did they feel?

   _____

   _____

_____

_____

More seriously...

4. This lesson stated that one of our enemy's primary strategies is to isolate and destroy. Satan always tries to divide married couples. He rejoices when we allow walls to develop in our relationships that prevent us from connecting. Do you agree with this? Why or why not? What are some strategies the enemy uses to divide couples?

_____

_____

_____

_____

5. The lesson gave the example of Joshua Chamberlain and the 20th Maine at the Battle of Gettysburg. What practical marriage applications can we draw from the example of Chamberlain's refusal to surrender ground to the enemy despite overwhelming conditions?

_____

_____

_____

_____

6. Why did God not intend for mankind to know evil? How has mankind been impacted by the experiential knowledge of evil?

What are some evil things, which will affect your marriage if you allow yourself to "know" them? How can you safeguard your marriage from these things?

_____

_____

_____

_____

7. Sin had a devastating impact on Adam and Eve's marriage as well as their relationship with God. How does sin affect your relationship with God? How does it affect your relationship with your spouse? What steps can you take to protect both relationships?

_____

_____

_____

_____

Prayer Time:

Theme Thought: Sin is destructive to your life and your marriage.

- Thank God that when you confess your sins, He is faithful and just to forgive you your sins and to cleanse you from all unrighteousness. (I Jn. 1:9)
- Ask the Holy Spirit to convict you of any unconfessed sin in your life. {You may want to use the Scripture verse below.}
- Confess any sin that the Holy Spirit brings to your attention.
- Ask the Holy Spirit to show you any way you have sinned against your spouse.
- Confess anything that the Holy Spirit brings to your attention.
- Ask God help you to be sensitive to sin in your life and your marriage relationship.

Examine me, O LORD, and prove me; Try my mind and my heart. (Ps. 26:2)

Search me, O God, and know my heart; Try me, and know my anxieties; (Ps. 139:23-24)

And see if there is any wicked way in me, And lead me in the way everlasting.

If we confess our sins, He is faithful and just to forgive us our sins and to cleanse us from all unrighteousness. (1 John 1:9)

3

A Proper Perspective on Marriage

Almost no one is foolish enough to imagine that he automatically deserves great success in any field of activity; yet almost everyone believes that he automatically deserves success in marriage.

Syndey J. Harris
(American Journalist, 1917-1986)

One time during the first year that my wife, Wendy, and I were married, we decided to go for a hike. We ended up in the middle of Victory Bog, a large swamp in northeastern Vermont. We didn't have a trail to show us the way out or a compass. (This was long before the personal GPS or cell phone.) Everything looked the same in every direction. All we could see was water, trees, and marshy ground all around us. I led us in the direction I thought would lead us to safety; however, in reality, I was leading us deeper into the bog. After what seemed like ages of trudging through muck and mire, we realized the sun was beginning to set. In final desperation, I turned around and led Wendy in the one direction we hadn't tried. My sense of direction told me that was the wrong way, but we were running out of time. In a short time, we came to higher ground. Before long we out of the bog. My sense of direction had been leading us away from where we really wanted to go the whole time.

Marriage can sometimes feel like our experience in Victory Bog. You think you know what marriage is all about and you think you know what you should do. You keep trudging along, doing what you've been doing, and you end up feeling more and more lost. Many people get so confused and lost in their marriages that they give up and leave their relationships.

When we were lost in the bog, one thing could have helped us find our way out. If I had a compass, I would have easily found our way out of that swamp. I knew that we needed to head west to get to high ground; however, I had no way to determine which way was west. A simple compass would have given us direction and given us a proper perspective on our position.

We need a proper perspective and understanding of marriage. God has already given us the perfect compass to guide us in our marriage. His compass enables us to properly understand marriage as He designed it. That compass is God's Word. Through His Word, God enables us to have a correct understanding of the marriage relationship.

1. In our society, what are some reasons that people commonly get married?

_____

_____

_____

_____

2. Do you think these are valid reasons for getting married? Why or why not?

_____

_____

_____

_____

If we find that the same kinds of challenges face every marriage, we might assume that God designed a purpose in this challenge that transcends something as illusionary as happiness... What if God designed marriage to make us holy more than to make us happy?

Gary Thomas
Sacred Marriage, Zondervan

The LORD God fashioned into a woman the rib which He had taken from the man, and brought her to the man.

The man said, "This is now bone of my bones, and flesh of my flesh; She shall be called Woman, Because she was taken out of Man."

For this reason a man shall leave his father and his mother, and be joined to his wife; and they shall become one flesh. (Gen. 2:22-24 NASB; italics added)

We have looked at these verses before. However, this time I want to focus on the three words at the beginning of verse 24, "for this reason". God had a purpose in creating marriage. I believe that God's purpose in marriage was much more than procreation and the continuation of the human race. God intended that in the marriage relationship a man and woman would be united spiritually, emotionally and physically. This connected relationship would take precedence over every other human relationship. As important as the parent-child relationship is, the marriage relationship is even more important. Even though Adam and Eve did not have human parents, God made sure they understood their marriage was more important than any other relationship. The husband's deepest emotional, social and physical needs would now be met in his wife. The wife's deepest needs would be met in her husband. Together this union would glorify God and bring joy to His heart.

3. What do you think are some of God's purposes for creating marriage?

_____

_____

_____

_____

Read Matthew 19:3-8; Mark 10:2-9.

When the Pharisees tested Jesus by bringing up the controversial subject of divorce, Jesus referred to the previously mentioned verses in Genesis 2. Jesus points out that divorce was never part of God's plan for marriage. God's purpose for marriage was the uniting of one man and one woman into an indivisible whole. This is God's marriage equation: $1 + 1 = 1$.

4. How does God's purpose in marriage (Gen. 2:22-24) relate to divorce?

_____

_____

_____

_____

I want to pause for a minute and clarify that it is not my intention to "beat up" on those who are divorced. Even in these passages in Matthew and Mark, Jesus recognized that divorce sometimes happened. In today's culture, divorce is even more prevalent than it was in Jesus' day. God never stops loving and caring for His children, whether they are single, married or divorced. However, we do need to realize that divorce is never part of God's perfect plan. Divorce is always damaging to everyone involved. According to Malachi 2:16, God hates divorce, because it is so destructive. However, He never hates divorced people.

> Therefore, whether you eat or drink, or whatever you do, do all to the glory of God. (1 Cor. 10:31)

I believe that the ultimate purpose of marriage is to bring glory to God. This is the transcending purpose of all creation. God created the universe so that He might be glorified. This is the grand purpose of our lives now and for all eternity. The purpose of my life is to bring glory to God. The purpose for your life is to bring glory to God. The purpose for our marriages is to bring glory to God. In the above verse, the Apostle Paul says that everything we do should be done for God's glory. I believe that includes the way we treat our respective spouses and the way we live our marriage relationships. There is no higher purpose for marriage than for me to glorify God in my marriage relationship. There is no greater purpose for your marriage either. When God created marriage, He intended that this unique joining of two individuals in a connected relationship would bring Him glory.

5. How do you think God wants a couple to glorify Him in their marriage?

_____

_____

_____

_____

> And *whatever* you do in word or deed, *do* all in the name of the Lord Jesus, giving thanks to God the Father through Him.

Wives, submit to your own husbands, as is fitting in the Lord.

Husbands, love your wives and do not be bitter toward them. (Col. 3:17-19 NJKV)

Let every detail in your lives--words, actions, whatever--be done in the name of the Master, Jesus, thanking God the Father every step of the way.

Wives, understand and support your husbands by submitting to them in ways that honor the Master.

Husbands, go all out in love for your wives. Don't take advantage of them. (Col. 3:17-19 *the Message*)

And whatever you do, do it heartily, as to the Lord and not to men, knowing that from the Lord you will receive the reward of the inheritance; for you serve the Lord Christ. (Col. 3:23-24 NKJV)

Everything that we do, we are to do thankfully and heartily to the Lord. I believe that this includes how we live out our marriage relationship. Every day I need to thank God for my wife. Each of us is to view our spouse as a special gift from God and be thankful for him or her. It is not okay for me to be lazy or lackadaisical in my marriage. I am to live out my marriage "heartily". What does that mean? It means that I am passionate about and committed to my relationship with my wife. Nothing, outside of my relationship with God, is more important to me than that marriage. That was not always the case.

Before I was married, I was passionate about hunting and fishing. I hunted almost every day from the opening day of the small game season to the close of deer season. During the spring and summer, I fished at least every other day. When I got married, I planned to continue my passionate pursuit of fish and game. Although Wendy never complained, I soon came to realize that she did not enjoy my time away from her and, eventually, from our family. God convicted me about my priorities. Although I still enjoy fishing and hunting when I can, nothing brings me more joy than spending time with my wife.

We meet with dozens of couples every year. Husbands and wives often have a passion for all kinds of activities. Some of the most common are sports, cars, boats, scrapbooking and social networking, just to name a few. Although there is nothing intrinsically wrong with these activities, usually each person lacks that same passion for his marriage. No activity is more worthy of our passion and commitment than our marriages.

Developing a passionate, caring relationship with your spouse takes commitment. You must prioritize your marriage. Husband, ultimately you don't love your wife sacrificially because she deserves it, you do it for the Lord. Wife, you don't support and submit to your husband because he deserves it, you do it for the Lord. Regardless of how your spouse responds, someday Jesus will reward you.

Our heavenly Father intends marriage to be the practical laboratory where we learn to live like Jesus. My wife does not have a perfect husband. Although I think she is pretty close, my wife isn't perfect either. I guarantee that your spouse is not perfect. As a matter of fact, your spouse is married to an imperfect person as well. God knew that none of our marriages would be perfect, because none of us are perfect. He wants us to learn to love and care for our spouses regardless of their short-comings. Marriage is the perfect laboratory to learn Christ-likeness. If we can learn to respond to and live with our respective spouses in a Christ-honoring way, regardless of what they do or don't do, then it will be easier for us treat other people the way Jesus wants us to treat them.

6. Do you agree or disagree that God wants you be thankful for your marriage and your spouse? _____ Why?

_____

_____

_____

_____

7. Do you agree or disagree that God wants you be passionate and committed in your marriage? _____ Why?

_____

_____

_____

_____

Read Ephesians 5:22-33 and Revelation 19:6-9.

God has another special purpose for marriage. He uses marriage to illustrate the relationship between Jesus and his body, the church. Jesus could have chosen some other relationship to portray His relationship to His church. He could have used the master-slave relationship or the parent-child relationship or the employer-employee relationship, but He didn't. The one relationship in the world that best describes the intimate relationship between the Savior and those for whom He died, is the marriage relationship. The church of Christ is described as His bride. The bride is described as being "arrayed in fine linen, clean and bright". Jesus dresses His bride in purity and radiance, like His own splendor and glory. There is something special and beautiful about every bride. Christ's bride will surpass every other bride because the Groom literally laid down His life for his wife.

Think about that for a moment. The marriage relationship is so important to God and so close to His heart that no other illustration would do justice to the love Jesus has for His people. No other relationship could describe the intimacy Jesus desires to have with us every day. Nothing else could appropriately describe the connected relationship and closeness that we will enjoy with Christ for all eternity.

Marriage is extremely important to God. For all eternity, we as believers will be in a marriage relationship. No, we will no longer be married to our earthly spouse (Matt. 22:35; Mark 12:25; Luke 20:35); however, we will enjoy an intimate, connected relationship with our Lord and Savior. God wants our present marriage to be preparing us for our eternal marriage relationship.

8. God uses the illustration of marriage to describe the relationship between Jesus Christ and His church. How does the Bible's use of marriage in this way give special value to the present institution of marriage?

_____

_____

_____

_____

9. How do you think your present marriage can prepare you for your eternal relationship with Jesus?

_____

_____

_____

_____

Read 1 Corinthians 7:2-5.

Often people get married hoping that marriage will meet their social, emotional and physical needs. Men especially often look forward to marriage in order to have their sexual needs fulfilled. Women often look forward to marriage to have their emotional needs met and have someone that can love and care for them. There is nothing essentially wrong in either of these desires. However, God's purpose in marriage is very different.

God designed marriage to be the place for the husband to unselfishly focus on the wife to meet her needs. God calls the husband to put the wife's welfare before his own. God also designed marriage to be the place where the wife unselfishly focuses on the husband to meet his needs. He also calls the wife to put her husband's needs before her own.

God's design for marriage is to be a loving relationship, where each person is putting the needs of his/her spouse before his/her own needs. This really shouldn't be surprising to us. Jesus tells us to show unselfish love to our neighbors and our enemies (Matt. 5:43, 44; 19:19; 22:39; Mark 12:31; Luke 10:27). So regardless of the condition of your marriage, you are responsible to put your spouse before yourself.

This passage in I Corinthians refers particularly to the sexual relationship in marriage. It says that our bodies belong to our spouse and are for our respective spouses only. Men, that includes your eyes, meaning what you look at. Your eyes are only for your wife. She should be the only woman you desire. Make sure that you do everything possible to guard your eyes against anything or anyone that would arouse desires that should only be for your wife. Women, this means that your body is only for your husband. Dress modestly in public but be willing to dress seductively in private for the enjoyment of your husband alone. Husband, your body belongs to your wife. Wife, your body belongs to your husband. That being said, remember what we already said, we are each responsible to put the needs and desires of our spouses before ourselves. That means never pressuring our spouse to meet our sexual needs. Husbands, there will be times that our wives are tired or not feeling well. We need to care for them and put their needs first at those times. As in every other aspect of the marriage relationship, in the bedroom, I need to focus on meeting my wife's needs and pleasing her sexually. At the same time, she focuses on meeting my needs. The result is that we enjoy a wonderfully fulfilling sexual relationship. That is what God intended for every aspect of the marriage relationship.

God does end this section by discussing a temporary hiatus in a couple's sexual relationship. If a couple decides together to temporarily forgo their sex life in order to focus on God and grow in their spiritual life, God says that is okay. However, even then God puts certain restrictions on their abstention from a sexual relationship. There must be a mutual agreement, and it must only be for a short, designated period of time. God knows that He created us sexual beings and how easily Satan can tempt us, especially during a period of chastity. Such designated times can help a couple grow in the spiritual element of their marriage relationship, as well as their personal walk with God, as long as they follow God's restrictions.

10. Think back to your engagement before you were married. Why did you want to marry your spouse?

_____

_____

_____

What did you think you would get from the marriage relationship?

_____

_____

_____

What did you think you would give your spouse?

_____

_____

_____

11. What do you think your spouse needs in your relationship?

_____

_____

_____

12. Do you know how to meet your spouse's needs? _____
If so, how do you do that?

_____

_____

_____

13. {Couples Exercise} Ask your spouse this question: *On a scale of 1 to 10, how well do I meet your needs?*
Write his/her answer here:

_____

Tell your spouse this: *I want to meet your needs. I want you to be able to share your deepest needs with me. I want to care about those needs. I want you to feel totally loved by me. Would you like that?*
Write his/her response here:

_____

Pray with your spouse: *Jesus, I thank You for giving me (spouse's name). I know that he/she is a special gift from you. Help me to value him/her every day. Help me to focus on (spouse's name) and meet his/her deepest needs. Thank You, Jesus, that you will help me to do that. I need wisdom in order to care for (spouse's name) and meet his/her needs. You promise that if I ask You for wisdom You will give it to me liberally. (Jam. 1:5) Today I'm asking for that wisdom, Jesus. Help me to truly put my husband's/wife's needs before my own.*

I ask this in Your name, Jesus. Amen

Review:

Use your sanctified imagination to answer these questions.

1. How well do you think Adam and Eve understood God's purpose for marriage? How do you think they viewed their marriage relationship before they sinned? How do you think they viewed their marriage after they sinned?

   _____

   _____

   _____

   _____

2. We know that at least one of Jesus's disciples was married. Peter had a wife. (Mark 1:30; Luke 4:38) It is possible that others could have also been married. How do you think a married disciples' relationship with Jesus would have impacted his relationship with his wife?

   _____

   _____

   _____

   _____

More seriously...

3. If the ultimate purpose of marriage is to bring glory to God, what does that mean for your marriage? How does God want to be glorified in your marriage relationship?

_____

_____

_____

_____

4. How can you live out your role as husband or wife thankfully and heartily to the Lord? How can you demonstrate your thankfulness to your spouse?

_____

_____

_____

_____

5. How does God want you to prioritize your marriage? How can you demonstrate that to your husband or wife?

_____

_____

_____

_____

6. We have seen that God values marriage so much that He uses it to illustrate the close relationship between Jesus Christ and His church. On a scale of 1 to 10, how much do you value your

marriage? _____ On a scale of 1 to 10, how much do you think God values your marriage? _____ Is there anything that God wants you to do to increase your appreciation for your marriage and your spouse?

_____

_____

_____

_____

7. We also saw that God's purpose for the husband is to put his wife's needs before his own and God's purpose for the wife is to put her husband's needs before her own. On a scale from 1 to 10, how well do you unselfishly seek to meet your spouse's needs? _____ How do you think God wants you to improve in this area?

_____

_____

_____

_____

_____

Prayer Time:

Theme Thought: God has a higher purpose in marriage than just my happiness.

- Praise God for marriage in general and your marriage in particular.
- Ask Jesus to show you any way that you have not appreciated your spouse and valued your marriage.
- Confess anything that Jesus brings to mind.
- Ask Jesus to reveal to you your spouse's good qualities.
- Thank God for your spouse. Specifically, thank God for those things that Jesus brought to your mind.
- Ask God to help you to be sensitive to your spouse and to put his/her needs before your own.

4

A Proper Attitude Toward
my Spouse, Part one

*Everything can be taken from a man but one thing: To choose
one's attitude in any given set of circumstances, to choose
one's way.*

Viktor Frankl
(Concentration Camp Survivor)

Our attitude is all important. Several years ago, I went through a difficult
time. I was dealing with some health problems, which were discouraging.
I was struggling with some issues on our church elder board of which I
am a member. We work for a small faith-based ministry, so finances were
also very tight. I also heard that some person was spreading lies about our
ministry. I was feeling very discouraged and had a very negative attitude.
My loving wife tried her best to help me, but couldn't get through to
me. I was seriously considering leaving the elder board and looking for a
second job.

Then one day, God got my attention. I was having my personal quiet
time with the Lord, reading His Word and praying, and He convicted me
of my bad attitude. It was as though God told me, "All you focus on are
the negative things. What about all the ways I bless you every day. You
have forgotten all the blessings I give you."

I immediately realized that God was right. I repented of my negative
attitude and asked God to help me see His blessings every day. I shared

that with my wife Wendy, and we began making changes. For over five years now, every evening before we pray together, Wendy and I each share at least one blessing we saw that day. We also keep a written record of our blessings. Every day, we write down the blessing(s) we experienced the day before. It has become our tradition that at the end of every year, together we read through all our blessings from that year. It reminds us of God's faithfulness and His goodness to us throughout the year.

This simple exercise of focusing on God's blessings totaling changed my attitude. The other people and the situations didn't really change. I changed because my attitude changed.

I share this as a simple illustration of the importance of having the right attitude. This is especially important in marriage. First, let's look at what God's Word says in general about our attitudes. Then, we'll look specifically at the importance of the right attitude in marriage.

> Is there any encouragement from belonging to Christ? Any comfort from his love? Any fellowship together in the Spirit? Are your hearts tender and compassionate? Then make me truly happy by *agreeing wholeheartedly* with each other, loving one another, and working together with one mind and purpose. Don't be selfish; don't try to impress others. Be humble, thinking of others as better than yourselves. Don't look out only for your own interests, but take an interest in others, too.
>
> You must have the same *attitude* that Christ Jesus had. Though he was God, he did not think of equality with God as something to cling to. Instead, he gave up his divine privileges; he took the humble position of a slave and was born as a human being. When he appeared in human form, he humbled himself in obedience to God and died a criminal's death on a cross. (Phil. 2:1-8 NLT; italics added)

The word translated *attitude* in Philippians 2:5 literally means a state of mind and understanding that affects the feelings. We cannot control our emotions; however, we can exert control over our thoughts. The way we think affects our feelings because our thoughts and feelings are intrinsically connected. What I choose to think about affects my emotions, and my feelings affect my thoughts.

Jesus, of course, was our perfect example of self-sacrificing love and humility. He, the perfect God and omnipotent Creator, was willing to humble Himself, in order to die for you and me. Where did that humbling process of Jesus begin? It began with His attitude. Because He had a humble, loving attitude, Jesus was able to lay aside His pre-incarnate glory and lower Himself to the position of a slave, in order to die for us. These verses describe the humbling process to which Jesus submitted Himself.

- He humbled Himself by being willing to set aside His divine attributes and glory.
- He humbled Himself by actually giving up His divine privileges.
- He willing took the position of a slave.
- He humbled Himself by becoming a human with a created body.
- He humbled Himself to completely obeying His Father.
- Then, He humbled Himself by dying the death of a disgraced criminal.

This journey of humility began with the proper attitude. His attitude of humility enabled Jesus to complete every humble act necessary for our redemption.

1. Our attitude is connected to our thoughts and our emotions. What things do you think Jesus thought about as He prepared to enter the world as a man?

_____

_____

_____

_____

2. What emotions do you think Jesus felt?

_____

_____

_____

_____

3. How did Jesus demonstrate His humble attitude during the 33 years that He lived on Earth?

_____

_____

_____

_____

The word translated _agreeing wholeheartedly_ in Philippians 2:2 is actually the very same word translated _attitude_ in verse 5. Everything described is verses 1 – 4, begins with having the proper attitude. Being able to agree wholeheartedly with my brothers and sisters in Christ depends on my attitude. My ability to love them and work together in unity depends on my attitude. My ability to not be selfish and not be proud, depends on whether or not I have a humble attitude. My ability to focus on others and actually put them before myself is dependent on my attitude. When my attitude is wrong, it is impossible for me to respond properly to others.

4. What are some ways that you have experienced your attitude affecting your interactions and relationships with other believers?

_____

_____

My attitude affects my actions. In order for the church to be the loving, unified body Jesus intended for it to be, each believer must have a truly humble attitude. This is true in the body of Christ and it is especially true in a marriage relationship. Let's see what we can learn from this passage in Philippians 2 that can assist each of us in our respective marriages.

First, what does God want a marriage to look like? Let's take another look at Philippians 2:1-8 from the perspective of marriage. Marriage is to be the one human relationship, more than any other that should be an encouraging relationship based on mutual faith in Christ (v. 1). A husband and wife are to enjoy a comforting and loving relationship based on Christ's love for them (v. 1). They are to enjoy real unity, empowered by the Holy Spirit who indwells them (v1.). Their hearts are to be tender and compassionate toward each other (v. 1). When they make decisions, the husband and wife are to agree wholeheartedly with each other, moving ahead to do what God leads them to do together (v. 2). They are to work together in their marriage with loving unity and Christ-centered goals (v. 2).

This type of marriage is only possible as both the husband and wife develop a Christ-like attitude toward his or her spouse. This attitude must be unselfish, willing to put the needs of his or her spouse first (v. 3). There must be genuineness, openness, and transparency in the relationship (v. 3). This means that each person must develop a humble attitude that conveys to his or her spouse that he or she is approachable and eager to listen. Each must determine to respond humbly to his or her spouse no matter what (v. 3). That is true humility. The husband must demonstrate by his attitude that he truly values and appreciates his wife (v. 3). The wife must also do the same for her husband. Each must have a caring attitude that allows him or her to actively enjoy those things that make his or her spouse happy (v. 4). Both the husband and wife need to intentionally put the interests of his or her spouse before his or her own, as well as learning to take an interest in what interests his or her spouse.

Wendy and I have learned to not only take an interest in each other's hobbies but actually to enjoy them together. My creative wife loves making quilts. I have learned not only to enjoy the beauty of her creations but to join her in the process. She asks my advice about possible patterns. We go to fabric stores together to choose the material. I've learned to enjoy giving input and being involved in the process. On my part, my favorite hobbies involve hunting and fishing. Wendy actually enjoys going to sporting goods stores with me to look at hunting and fishing gear. She asks me questions, and I enjoy explaining the uses for various items. When I go fishing, Wendy likes to come along. She brings a chair, her book, and a camera. While I fish, she enjoys relaxing outdoors, reading, taking photos, or asking me questions about fishing flies or lures. At home, we have a room set up with a sewing station for Wendy to work on her quilts and a fly tying station where I make my flies for fishing. We enjoy being together while we are also enjoying our very different hobbies.

5. How have you experienced a negative attitude affecting your marriage relationship?

_____

_____

_____

_____

6. How have you experienced a positive attitude affecting your marriage relationship?

_____

_____

_____

_____

7. For your part, what is necessary in order to have a humble, positive attitude toward your spouse?

_____

_____

_____

_____

8. How can you take an interest in what interests your husband or wife?

_____

_____

_____

_____

The only way it is possible to fulfill these responsibilities in a marriage relationship is by having the same humble attitude as Jesus (Phil. 2:5). Not only is Jesus our perfect example, but He also wants to help each of us also develop that same humble attitude. He has promised to never leave us on our own (John 14: 16-18; Heb. 13:5). Jesus also promises to answer our prayers (John 14:14; 16:23, 24). Jesus Himself is constantly praying for us (Rom. 8:26; Heb. 7:25). He empathizes and cares about our struggles (Heb. 4:14-16). Jesus promises to give us wisdom if we simply ask for it (James 1:5). The wisdom that He gives us is peaceful, gentle, unselfish, merciful and fair (James 3:17). This wisdom will be displayed in our attitude and our actions.

So how do I develop the humble attitude that I need to have towards my wife? The only way I can do it is with the help of my loving Savior. There are five practical steps I can take in order to develop a genuine Christ-like attitude toward Wendy. This list is not all-inclusive, but it offers some valid recommendations for transforming my attitude towards Wendy. These steps will also help any husband or wife, who will commit to putting them into practice.

- My relationship with Jesus Christ must be a priority in my life. I must be spending time with Jesus every day, reading His Word and talking with Him. As I have a closely connected relationship with Him, Jesus will change my attitude toward my wife.
- I need to confess and repent of any sin in my life. Any sin will affect my attitude toward my wife. Unconfessed sin will keep me from connecting with Jesus and my wife. It will cause walls in our relationship. So I will not have the right attitude if I am harboring any sin.
- I must pray often for Jesus to reveal where my attitude is wrong and show me how to develop a proper attitude toward my wife. I don't always know when I am indulging in a bad attitude; however, Jesus always knows. He will prompt me when and show me how my attitude is wrong if I ask Him to do so. He will also help me to do what I need to do in order to change my attitude.
- I need to intentionally look for opportunities to put my wife's needs and desires before my own. I can take an interest in the things that interest her. As I do this, I need to ask Jesus to help me demonstrate a loving, caring attitude towards Wendy that enables me to focus on her. Focusing on her means really enjoying putting her first. My attitude will show my wife if I really want to do this or if I am just going through the motions because it is what I am supposed to do. If I am not really interested and don't enjoy putting Wendy first, she will not feel loved and valued, rather she will feel like a burden. So I need Jesus to help me demonstrate the right attitude as I intentionally focus on my wife.
- My attitude is irrevocably connected to my thoughts. So I must be quick to recognize and reject negative thoughts toward my spouse. As soon as I recognize that I am struggling with a negative thought, I must ask Jesus to remove that thought and fill my mind with His thoughts. That will help me to replace the negative with positive thoughts towards my wife. I can pause and thank Jesus for

Wendy and ask Him to give me a fresh appreciation for her. I can ask Jesus to help me view her as His special daughter for whom He gave His life. I can intentionally focus my thoughts on Wendy's gifts and strengths. These steps will help to redirect my thoughts and, as a result, change my attitude.

9. Do you agree that a close relationship with Jesus is important to have a good attitude toward your spouse?_____ Why or why not?

_____

_____

_____

_____

10. Do you agree that sin affects your relationship with your spouse? _____ Why or why not?

_____

_____

_____

_____

11. How can prayer help you have a better attitude toward your spouse?

_____

_____

_____

_____

Read: Philippians 4:4-8.

Our thoughts always influence our attitude. That fact is evident in this passage in Philippians 4. It begins with rejoicing in our personal relationship with the Lord. When I am enjoying a close, connected relationship with Jesus, it will affect my thoughts and my attitude. Both my thoughts and attitude will be positive. Then it will be much easier for me to enjoy my human relationships, especially my relationship with my wife.

In verse 5, the word translated *gentleness* or *gentle spirit* or *moderation*, depending on the Bible translation you are reading, actually means appropriate. In other words, we are to always respond appropriately to the situation. We don't overreact, but we also don't fail to act when action is required. Jesus was the perfect example of always responding perfectly in every situation. As I remember that *the Lord is at hand* or Jesus is always there with me, I can respond appropriately. I can ask Jesus to help me respond correctly and demonstrate the proper attitude in every situation. Usually, the proper response is to be gentle and longsuffering because responding angrily doesn't please God (James 1:19, 20). This is especially important in the marital relationship.

In verse 6, we are encouraged to not give into anxiety for any reason. It is never God's will for His children to be anxious. Anxiety is a weed that seeks to spread its tendrils through our hearts and minds. Anxiety can easily damage my heart, control my thoughts, and influence my attitude if I allow it to do so. The weedicide that will stop that from happening is prayer. Rather than surrendering to anxiety, I need to talk to Jesus about my anxious feelings and thoughts. I focus on the many blessings He has given me and begin to thank Him. I can ask Jesus to remove those anxious feelings and thoughts and replace them with something good. Doing this will stop my anxious thoughts before they can infect my attitude and then be passed on to others, like my wife.

Verse 7 tells us the result of praying rather than surrendering to anxiety. We will experience God's supernatural peace. God's peace is beyond our understanding or comprehension because it doesn't depend on our circumstances. That same peace actually guards our hearts and minds from harmful thoughts, feelings, and attitudes. The word translated *guard* actually means to protect by a military guard to prevent hostile invasion. The enemy is constantly attempting to attack us with negative thoughts or feelings, which then affect our attitudes. When we are experiencing God's peace, our thoughts and emotions are safe, regardless of the situation. Divine peace fills our minds and hearts, which in turn is evident in our attitudes.

Verse 8 stresses the importance of controlling what I focus my thoughts upon. Paul gives 8 criteria for our thoughts. When our thoughts meet these criteria they will be glorifying to God. Then our attitudes will also glorify Him.

How does this affect my marriage and my relationship with my wife?

- I need a close relationship with Jesus. I need to be connecting with Him every day and rejoicing in Him.
- I need to ask Jesus to help me respond correctly to my wife in every situation. As I remember that Jesus is there with me, I need to check my attitude before I respond to Wendy. I might want to imagine Jesus standing behind Wendy when I talk to her. I need to remember that my wife is His beloved daughter. I can ask Jesus to help my tone of voice and demeanor be open, caring, and understanding.
- I need to examine my emotions and identify any fear or anxiety. Then I simply talk to Jesus about anything making me fearful or anxious. I can pray and release those things to Jesus as I picture myself placing them in His hands and letting go. I can ask Jesus to put something good in my life in place of those fears and anxieties. Then I ask Him to fill my heart and mind with His peace.
- I can also pray for Wendy. I can ask Jesus to help her cast her cares on Him (1 Pet. 5:7). I can pray for Jesus to remove my wife's fears and anxieties and give her peace. I ask Jesus to safeguard our relationship with His peace.
- I ask Jesus to help the peace in my heart and mind overflow in my attitude toward my wife. I pray that my tone of voice, facial expression, words and emotions would display His peace as I relate to my wife. I ask Him to help my heart move towards my wife and care about her, regardless of her words or her response. Jesus can help me unselfishly focus on Wendy to care

about her. I pray that she will feel safe in opening her heart to me and truly feel loved by me.

- I need to guard the things I think about. I must refuse to focus my mind on anything that doesn't meet the criteria of Philippians 4:8. I ask Jesus to help me identify and reject wrong thoughts. I also ask Him to help me focus on the right thoughts about Wendy. Thinking good things about my wife will affect my attitude toward her and make our relationship stronger. Thinking bad things will also affect my attitude in a negative way and damage our relationship. My attitude will be evident to my wife in my tone of voice, facial expression, and posture, as well as my words and actions. I can pray and commit my thoughts and attitude to Jesus. I can ask Him to help me build up and encourage my wife through my words, actions, and attitude.

12. Do you think rejoicing in the Lord really will have any effect on your marriage?_____
    Why or why not?

_____

_____

_____

_____

13. How might fear or anxiety affect your marriage?

_____

_____

_____

_____

14. How could you demonstrate God's peace toward your spouse?

_____

_____

_____

_____

15. {Personal Exercise} Spend some time alone with the Lord asking Him the following questions.

Jesus, is there anything that is keeping me from enjoying and rejoicing in my relationship with you?

If Jesus brings any sin to your mind, confess it and ask His forgiveness.

If He brings anything else to your mind, simply talk to Jesus about it and give it to Him.

Jesus, please show me, if I have any fear or anxiety in my life.

If Jesus brings anything to mind, simply talk to Him about it and release it to Him.

Jesus, please put good things in my life, in place of that fear and anxiety.

Jesus, what kind of thoughts do you want me to think towards (spouse's name)? *Jesus, help me reject wrong thoughts and focus on the right thoughts towards (spouse's name).*

Jesus, what kind of attitude do you want me to have towards (spouse's name)? *Jesus, please help me demonstrate the right attitude towards (spouse's name) at all times. Help my tone*

of voice, facial expression and posture show (spouse's name)
that I really care about him/her. Help my words and actions
also show (spouse's name) that I care.

I ask this in Your name, Jesus. Amen

Review:

Use your sanctified imagination to answer these questions.

1. Imagine that you were in heaven when it was time for God the Son to come to earth. For the first time, the eternal, omnipotent Creator will be confined to a tiny body in the womb of a virgin girl. What do you think the scene in heaven was like? What thoughts and emotions might you have felt if you had been there?

    _____

    _____

    _____

    _____

2. Imagine that you were in heaven when Jesus returned from His time on earth. What do you think the scene in heaven was like then? What thoughts and emotions might you have felt if you had been there? How was the second scene different from the first?

    _____

    _____

    _____

    _____

More seriously…

3. How do you think God wants you to show a humble, Christ-like attitude toward your spouse?

_____

_____

_____

_____

4. How can you take an interest in the things that interest your spouse?

_____

_____

_____

_____

5. How do your thoughts and feelings affect your attitude toward your spouse? What effect does your attitude have on your marriage relationship?

_____

_____

_____

_____

6. How does Jesus want you to guard your thoughts toward your spouse?

_____

_____

_____

_____

Prayer Time:

Theme Thought: God wants me to have a humble, Christ-like attitude toward my spouse.

- Thank Jesus for being willing to humble Himself and die for you.
- Ask Jesus to show you any way that you have demonstrated a wrong attitude toward your spouse.
- Confess anything that He brings to mind.
- Ask Jesus how He wants you to take an interest in your spouse and the things he/she enjoys?

- Ask Jesus to reveal any fear, anxiety or wrong thoughts that you are harboring?
- If Jesus brings anything to mind, release it to Him and ask Him to put good things in place of those fears, anxieties or wrong thoughts.
- Ask Jesus to guard your thoughts and emotions, especially towards your spouse.
- Ask Jesus to help you demonstrate a humble, Christ-like attitude toward your spouse.

5

A Proper Attitude Toward my Spouse, Part Two

The noted English architect Sir Christopher Wren was supervising the construction of a magnificent cathedral in London. A journalist thought it would be interesting to interview some of the workers, so he chose three and asked them this question, "What are you doing?" The first replied, "I'm cutting stone for 10 shillings a day." The next answered, "I'm putting in 10 hours a day on this job." But the third said, "I'm helping Sir Christopher Wren construct one of London's greatest cathedrals."

Source Unknown

In the last chapter, we looked at the importance of having a humble, Christ-like attitude toward our spouse. In the above illustration, you can see how three men doing the same job had vastly different attitudes. The third man is the only one who not only seemed to enjoy his job but also understood that he was actually participating in something great. A marriage relationship is grander and more valuable than any cathedral. Cathedrals are only temporary, while relationships last forever.

In this chapter, we want to continue studying the importance of your attitude as it relates to your marriage. We will be looking at the two of the most well-known Scripture passages dealing with marriage; however, we will be focusing on the attitudes necessary to fulfill the commands given to both husbands and wives in these Scriptures. The degree to which my marriage will succeed and thrive depends to a large degree on my attitude, as well as my wife's. Our attitudes toward each other, our roles in the relationship and our marriage helps determine the health of our marriage relationship. So let's continue to study the importance of the proper attitude in marriage.

Read: Ephesians 5:15-33.

At the beginning of this passage, Paul challenges the Ephesian believers to live wisely (v. 15) and use their time wisely (v. 16). He then encourages them to really comprehend or understand God's will (v. 17). In the verses that follow, the Apostle Paul relates some definite actions, which are always God's will for His children (vv. 18-33). Verses 18-21 are written to all believers and affect our relationships with others, including our respective spouses, and with God. Verses 22-33 are written specifically to husbands and wives. Let's take a look at the requisite attitudes necessary to fulfill all these actions in a marriage relationship.

The first thing we see is the importance of being filled with the Spirit or controlled by the Holy Spirit, rather than any addiction (v. 18). Addictions will always destroy relationships. There is always a reason that a person has an addiction. No one just gets up one day and decides, "I don' have anything else to do today, so I think I will go out and get addicted to drugs or pornography or gambling or food or shopping or the internet."

There are always three factors involved in any addiction:

1. Emotional – A person with an addiction is trying to cover emotional pain or meet an unmet emotional need.
2. Spiritual – An addiction is a spiritual stronghold in the person's life, which damages his/her relationship with God.
3. Physical – There is a physical reaction in the person's brain and body, which is pleasurable, at least for a time.

To experience freedom over any addiction the person must deal with all three factors. A good support system of caring believers is also important for this to take place. The help of a competent Christian counselor who understands how to help a person resolve these three issues may also be very helpful.

The first step to victory over addiction is committing to overcoming it and doing whatever is necessary for that to happen. Addiction will destroy a marriage.

Rather than giving into addiction, we are to be empowered by the Holy Spirit. Only then can we demonstrate the proper attitudes, thoughts, and actions toward our spouses.

1. Have you or your spouse ever struggled with any form of addiction? _____
    If so, how did it impact your relationships?

    _____

    _____

    _____

    _____

2. What steps, if any, have you or your spouse taken to resolve that addiction?

    _____

    _____

    _____

    _____

3. What steps are you personally willing to take to resolve any addiction impacting your marriage?

    _____

    _____

_____

_____

Ephesians 5:19 talks about the importance of music that glorifies God. Such music not only affects our relationship with God, but also affects our relationship with others. It also speaks to our own hearts and will therefore affect our attitude. Wendy can always tell when I'm sick or in a "bad mood" because I'm quiet. Usually, around the house, I'm singing, humming or whistling a hymn, praise song or kid's chorus, but I don't do that when I'm not doing well. Often when she points that out to me, as soon as I begin singing some God-honoring song, my spirits lift and my attitude changes. Try it the next time you feel "down".

Verse 20 reminds us of the importance of thanking God for everything. This isn't referring to simply thanking God before meals, it means having a continual heart attitude of gratitude. This means I'm truly thankful for God's gifts, especially my wife. So, a genuinely thankful attitude always affects how I speak to and act towards my wife.

4. For what three things about your spouse can you thank God today?

- _____

_____

- _____

_____

- _____

_____

Submitting to one another in the fear of God. (Eph. 5:21 NKJV)

Submit to one another out of reverence for Christ. (Eph. 5:21 NLT)

I find it very interesting that before Paul launches into this section of his letter dealing with roles and responsibilities in the home, he introduces the concept of mutual submission. The Greek word translated *submitting* means to subordinate, subject or put under. God, through Paul's quill, is encouraging us to willingly subordinate our own desires and needs under those of others. It is in a very real sense, it means me putting others before myself, which is exactly what Jesus taught repeatedly. (Matt. 20:25-28; Mark 9:35; 10:43-25) God intends for every church to be filled with believers who are continually putting others before themselves. We don't submit to another because of his or her person, position or popularity, but rather out of reverence to Christ who made that person. This is also what He desires for marriage. God calls husbands to put their respective wives needs before their own and He calls wives to do the same to their husbands. That is mutual submission. It is only possible when each of us has a humble, servant attitude toward our spouse. We willingly submit to each other out of our love and reverence for Jesus Christ.

5. {Personal Exercise} Spend some time alone with the Lord asking Him the following questions.

    Jesus, please, show me any way that I'm putting my desires and needs before (spouse's name).

    If Jesus brings anything to your mind, confess it and ask His forgiveness.

    Jesus, how do You want me to put (spouse's name)'s desires and needs before my own?

    Write down anything that Jesus tells you:

    _____

    _____

Jesus, thank you that You are there to help me. You can give
me the wisdom and ability to willingly put (spouse's name)
before myself. You can also help me to have a humble, servant
attitude as I do that. Remind me of this every day.

Thank You, Jesus. I ask this in Your name. Amen

In Ephesians 5:22-23, Paul specifically addresses wives, encouraging them to submit to their husbands. This isn't referring to the wife putting the husband's desires and needs before herself. We already dealt with that under the previous section and saw that this is the responsibility of both husband and wife. It doesn't mean that the wife just lets the husband make all the decisions and goes along with whatever he says. (We'll talk about decision making in a later chapter.) It doesn't mean that the wife has no voice in the marriage. However, it does mean that the wife willingly submits and supports the husband's leadership in the marriage and the family. This is only possible when the wife has a humble, submissive attitude toward her husband.

In verses 25 to 33, Paul commands husbands to love their wives with the same love Christ had for the Church. This means that the husband is responsible to demonstrate the same self-sacrificing love for his wife that Jesus demonstrated at the cross when He died for us. This doesn't just mean that the husband is willing to die for his wife, if necessary, it means he cares for her and cherishes her more than himself. The husband must be willing to sacrifice his own desires to care for his wife. A husband can only do this when he has a humble, caring attitude toward his wife.

In Ephesians 5:22-6:4, Paul describes the God-designed system of authority and responsibility in the family. Jesus Christ is at the ultimate head of the family. Then, the husband is responsible to be a loving, godly leader. The wife is responsible to support and assist the husband. The children are responsible to obey and honor their parents. God designed this system for the protection of each member of the family and to be a constant reminder of the relationship between Jesus and His Church. Each person can only fulfill his or her role in the family the way God intended by maintaining a Christ-like attitude.

6. Can you remember a time you acted selfishly in your marriage relationship? _____

   How did that affect your relationship?

   _____

   _____

   _____

   _____

7. Write down one time your spouse acted unselfishly in your relationship.

   _____

   _____

   _____

   _____

8. How did it make you feel when your spouse did that?

   _____

   _____

   _____

   _____

9. Personal Exercise} Spend some time alone with the Lord.

Jesus, You gave (spouse's name) to me as a special gift. You have called me to be a godly husband or wife (choose the one that applies). I understand that this is a very important responsibility. I need Your help to be the husband (or wife) that you want me to be.

Jesus, what things need to change in my life for me to be a godly husband (or wife)?

Write down anything that Jesus tells you:

_____

_____

_____

_____

Jesus, I also know that I need to have the right attitude to properly fulfill my role in our marriage and family. Jesus, please, show me if I am harboring any wrong attitudes towards my spouse or children.

If Jesus brings anything to your mind, confess it and ask His forgiveness.

Jesus, please show what kind of attitude You want me to have toward my husband/wife.

_____

_____

_____

_____

Jesus, thank You that You are eager to help me. With Your help, I can be the Husband/wife that You created me to be. Remind me of that every day

In Your name, amen.

Read: I Peter 3:1-8.

In these verses, Peter discusses the marriage relationship. In the first six verses, he addresses the responsibilities of the wife. Wives are again encouraged to develop a submissive attitude toward their respective husbands. That kind of godly attitude is demonstrated by a gentle, quiet spirit which flows out of a heart connection with God.

In the next verse, Peter challenges husbands to have an understanding attitude toward their wives. This means the husband desires to know and understand his wife at the deepest level: her struggles, her pain, her joys, and her heart. It also means the husband honors and values his wife as God values her.

Then Peter commands both husbands and wives to have attitudes of unity, sympathy, kindness, tenderness, and humility.

10. If you are a wife, read I Peter 3:1-6 several times. Possibly read it in different translations. Meditate on these verses for 5 minutes. Then, prayerfully consider the following questions:

- What kind of attitude is demonstrated by my actions toward my husband?
- If my husband was an unbeliever, would my attitude and actions cause him to want to accept Christ? Why or why not?
- Is there anything I need to change to develop and demonstrate a gentle quiet spirit?
- How do I need to change my attitude toward my husband?

Pray and ask Jesus to help you in these areas.

11. If you are a husband, read I Peter 3:7- 8 several times. Possibly read it in different translations. Meditate on these verses for 5 minutes. Then, prayerfully consider the following questions:

- What kind of attitude is demonstrated by my actions toward my wife?
- Does my wife feel understood by me? Why or Why not?
- Does my wife feel that I honor and value her? Why or why not?
- How do I need to change to be more understanding toward my wife?
- How do I need to change to develop a more sympathetic, caring, tender, and humble attitude toward my wife?

Pray and ask Jesus to help you in these areas.

As we have worked with couples over the years, we often see a reoccurring theme: wives who are dominant and husbands who are passive, especially in spiritual things. This is not true with every couple, but it is true in many marriages. We have already studied God's plan for marriage: the husband to be a loving leader and the wife to be the supportive helper. Why isn't that true in the majority of marriages, even Christian marriages?

I believe the reason is that marriage is under attack. The enemy is constantly doing all he can to destroy marriages and thwart God's plan. These attacks start when we are young. Often, children grow up in homes where the father is not a strong spiritual leader. Many times, the father is a very negative role model. Boys grow up not knowing how to be a biblical, godly leader. These husbands often abdicate their leadership to their wives. Girls are often damaged by abuse, which causes them to want to always be in control to protect themselves. When they get married, these women continue to dominate and control so they won't get hurt again. However, neither spouse enjoys and thrives in this type of marriage.

You can see how this kind of marriage relationship is the opposite of what God intended. The good news is that every couple can enjoy marriage the way God designed it. Knowing God's purpose and design for marriage is a beginning; however, it isn't enough to actually change our marriages. Marriages change as we change. The remainder of this book will deal with the practical application and exercises that will help these changes take place.

Review:

Use your sanctified imagination to answer these questions.

1. Imagine that Adam and Eve didn't sin and sin never entered the human race. How do you think husbands would act towards their wives? How would wives act toward their husbands? How would the parent's relationship affect their children?

    _____

    _____

    _____

    _____

2. We know from Scripture that Peter did have a wife at some point. Assuming that his wife was still alive at the time the New Testament was written, how do you think Peter might have treated her before he met Jesus? How do you think he treated her after knowing Jesus?

    _____

    _____

    _____

    _____

More seriously…

3. The author talked about "mutual submission." How do you think you and your spouse could demonstrate this in your relationship?

_____

_____

_____

_____

For wives…

4. How do you think the Lord wants you to develop a more humble, submissive attitude toward your husband?

_____

_____

_____

_____

5. How can you demonstrate that attitude to your husband?

_____

_____

_____

_____

For husbands...

6. How do you think the Lord wants you to develop a more self-sacrificing, caring and understanding attitude toward your wife?

_____

_____

_____

_____

7. How can you demonstrate that attitude to your wife?

_____

_____

_____

_____

Prayer Time:

Theme Thought: I need a humble, unselfish attitude toward my spouse in order to fulfill my role in my marriage.

- Thank Jesus for the gift of marriage.
- Thank Him for your spouse.
- Ask Jesus to show you how He wants you to put your spouse's needs before your own.
- Ask Jesus to show you any way that you have failed to properly fulfill your role in your marriage.
- Ask Jesus to forgive you for anything He brings to mind.
- Ask Jesus to show you one practical way that you can be a better husband/wife.
- Ask Jesus to show you any way that you need to change your attitude in order to be a better husband/wife.
- Ask Jesus to give you the strength and wisdom to follow through and make changes where necessary,

Section Two

Practical Projects
for Marriage

6

Taking off our Backpacks

In our younger days, Wendy and I enjoyed hiking and backpacking. We hiked in such places as West Virginia, New York, Vermont, New Hampshire, and even Alaska. When we were backpacking, we would become more and more eager to make camp as the day wore on. Usually, early in the day, the pack felt fairly light. However, as it got later in the day, our packs seemed to grow heavier and heavier. When we reached our camping spot, the first thing we did was take off our backpacks.

What we didn't realize when we got married was that we each brought a backpack into marriage with us. Every person has a backpack of "stuff" he or she brings into his marriage. Of course, I'm not talking about a literal backpack. However, the stuff we bring into marriage with us is very real.

Our backpacks may contain:

- Emotional Pain
- Abuse
- Poor Choices
- Poor Response Patterns
- Addictions
- Anger
- Depression
- Anxiety

This is not an all-inclusive list. Things that happened to us in the past leave lasting scars and effects. The things that impact us the most usually happened to us during childhood. John Regier, the founder and director of *Caring for the Heart Ministries* (Colorado Springs, CO), says, "Ninety percent of what we react to as adults is connected to childhood pain." When we are children, we are very vulnerable. People hurt us with words and actions and those things damage our hearts. As adults, we are more able to handle hurtful words or comments rationally. Children do not possess that ability. The things that hurt us most deeply are those that happened to us as children.

We grow up and think that we left those childhood hurts behind us. The truth is we are still carrying them around in our proverbial backpack. For instance, if you had an angry parent, you will probably struggle when you are around an angry person. If you were abused as a child, you will struggle in any situation that reminds you of the abuse. If you had a depressed parent, you may struggle when you are with a depressed person. These are just a few examples.

We all get married expecting the best of our spouse and our marriage. For a while, everything is wonderful, this is known as the "honeymoon" period. Usually, this lasts a few weeks or months, although I know one couple whose honeymoon period ended before they left the wedding reception. However, it is inevitable that the stuff in our backpacks will start to come out in very unhealthy ways. We call this "stepping on each other's pain." We all carry emotional pain from our past in our respective backpacks. Sooner or later, our spouses will touch that pain. Then, we usually respond in unhealthy ways that step on their pain. Then, they respond in a way that causes us more pain. We call this the "Vicious Cycle," and I will talk more about it later in this book. The good news is - there is a solution.

If any of you have ever used a two-person backpacking tent, you know how small such a tent is. They are made small on purpose so they are light to carry. There is just enough room inside for two to sleep. There is not enough room for two people wearing their backpacks. The packs have to come off. Then the two people can fit in the tent and spend a reasonably comfortable night in their sleeping bags.

The same is true in marriage. The backpacks have to come off. The only way that can happen is to work through the issues you each brought into your marriage. Ignoring emotional pain and issues from our past doesn't mean they go away. No, instead they become even more entrenched in our lives if we don't deal with them. The good news is that we can be free from those things. Freedom only comes from being willing to take an honest look at how we have been damaged and release the pain to Jesus. The purpose of this chapter is to help you take off your backpack by working through pain issues from your past.

Acknowledge the Pain

The first thing that we need to do is to admit how we have been hurt. It is not my intent to dishonor parents or others in any way. However, before we can resolve our emotional pain, we must be honest about the people who hurt us and the ways we were hurt. I can say with total confidence – none of us grew up in perfect homes. Not even Jesus had perfect earthly parents or siblings. Because Adam and Eve sinned before having children, no parents have ever been perfect. Even those who grow up in the best homes have parents who are still sinners with siblings who are sinners. They visit grandparents, uncles, aunts, and cousins who are all sinners. They go to school with classmates who are sinners and are taught by teachers who are sinners. This means that it is inevitable that everyone experiences emotional pain. Then they grow up and marry a sinner and have children who, you guessed it, are sinners. They get a job and work with sinners. They go to a church full of believers who are saved sinners. All of this causes more pain.

We can be damaged by two different types of pain. The most obvious kind of emotional pain is caused by the bad things that happened to someone. Examples are any kind of abuse, criticism, being bullied, unreasonable expectations, being drained emotionally or being dominated. The second kind of emotional pain is less obvious and it involves the good things that didn't happen to someone. We all have certain emotional needs. If those needs are not met, especially when we are children, we will be damaged. Examples are: not feeling loved, not feeling important, not being talked to, being ignored or not being appreciated. We all have experienced one of these types of emotional pain and some people have experienced both. The first step in getting this pain out of our lives and relationships is identifying how we have been hurt and by whom.

In the following charts, list each person that hurt you and how they hurt you. If necessary, use extra pieces of paper. See the examples in each chart.

Childhood	
Name:	**How this person hurt me:**
Dad	*His anger and expectations*

Adulthood	
Name:	**How this person hurt me:**
Boss	*His verbal abuse*
_____	_____
_____	_____
_____	_____
_____	_____
_____	_____
_____	_____
_____	_____
_____	_____
_____	_____
_____	_____
_____	_____
_____	_____
_____	_____
_____	_____
_____	_____
_____	_____
_____	_____
_____	_____
_____	_____

If you struggled with filling out these charts, take some time to pray. Ask Jesus to show you how your heart has been damaged. Then go back and write anything that Jesus revealed to you.

Now that you have identified those who caused you emotional pain, it is important to go one step farther. In the following charts, again write the same names of people that hurt you. Then, next to each name, write how it made you feel. For instance, in the previous chart I used *Dad* as a hypothetical example. Under "How this person hurt me" I wrote *his anger and expectations*. So in the chart below, I wrote *Dad* again and then wrote how his anger and expectations made me feel.

Childhood	
Name:	**How this person made me feel:**
Dad	*afraid, I felt I could never do anything right, not good enough*

Adulthood	
Name:	**How this person made me feel:**
Boss	*angry, I feel not valued*
_____	_____
_____	_____
_____	_____
_____	_____
_____	_____
_____	_____
_____	_____
_____	_____
_____	_____
_____	_____
_____	_____
_____	_____
_____	_____
_____	_____
_____	_____
_____	_____
_____	_____
_____	_____
_____	_____

Releasing the Pain

The next step is releasing all that pain that you listed in the previous charts. I often tell the people we counsel that I wish I could take their pain away and heal their hearts, but I can't do that. However, I know the One who can and so do you if you are a believer. Jesus cares about your pain. Luke 4:18 tells us that one of the reasons Jesus came to earth was to heal the brokenhearted. The Greek words used there actually mean crushed or shattered hearts. Jesus is still healing broken, crushed and shattered hearts today.

Jesus is waiting to take our emotional pain and heal our hearts if we will let Him. Jesus invites us to cast our cares and anxieties on Him because He cares about us. (I Pet. 5:7) The way we release our pain to Jesus is through prayer. Below is a prayer to help you pray through the emotional pain you identified and release it to Jesus. Using the previous lists, use this prayer to pray about each person who hurt you. Put the names and items you listed in the appropriate places in the prayer. Using the previous example, I would place *Dad* in the first set of parentheses, *his anger and expectations* in the second set and *afraid, that I couldn't do anything right and not good enough* in the third set. Pray this prayer for each person that you listed.

Jesus, I acknowledge that (Name of the person) has hurt me by his/her (How that person hurt you). This caused my heart to feel (How that person made you feel). Jesus, what did that do to my heart?

Pause and let Jesus speak to your heart.

Jesus, can you heal my heart from that pain?

Pause and let Jesus speak to your heart.

Jesus, I don't want to hold on to this pain any longer. It's too heavy and it hurts too much. Today, I want to place this pain in your hands and let it go. Jesus, do I need to forgive (Name of the person) or have I already done that?

Pause and let Jesus speak to your heart. If Jesus tells you to forgive, continue praying through the next section. If Jesus tells you that you have already forgiven him/her, go down to the * below.

Jesus, today I choose to forgive (Name of the person). I ask that You grant him/her grace, mercy and pardon just as You've given me. I am willing to take Your grace to pay for the emotional pain and consequences that (Name of the person) has caused me. I ask You to turn those consequences into blessings for

Your glory and for good in my life. I ask You, Lord, to take back any ground I gave to the enemy through my unforgiveness and bitterness. I yield that ground to Your control.

*Jesus, I've given You the pain that (Name of the person) has caused me and You have helped me to forgive him/her. Jesus, what do You want to put in my life in place of that pain?

Pause and let Jesus speak to your heart.

Thank You, Jesus, for taking my pain and replacing it with good things.

Thank You, Jesus. I ask this in Your name. Amen

Dealing with Sin

Besides pain, there is often something else that we carry in our backpack – sin. We all are born with a sin nature. Actually, Scripture tells us that we are sinners from conception. (Ps. 51:5) Many times we respond to emotional pain in the wrong ways. The pain is not our fault; however, the way we choose to respond is. Often, our response patterns are sinful.

We have two children, a boy and a girl who are only 18 months apart. They are both grown now, married, and have children of their own. However, when they were young, our daughter seemed to enjoy saying things that irritated her brother. His response was not to tell his sister that he loved her and ask her not to say those hurtful things. No, his immediate response was to hit her on the top of the head. Our daughter would be disciplined, but so would our son for the wrong way he responded.

Sometimes we sin as a response to pain. Sometimes we sin just because we are self-centered sinners. Even as believers, we often find ourselves sinning and doing what we don't want to do. (Rom. 7:17-25) Any kind of sin is a heavy weight in our backpacks and must be removed. We do that through praying, confessing our sin and accepting God's forgiveness.

> If we confess our sins, He is faithful and just to forgive us *our* sins and to cleanse us from all unrighteousness. (1 John 1:9)

Take some time to do a self-examination. Are you aware of any unconfessed sin in your life? After a period of time examining your own heart and life, pray the following prayer for each sin that you have identified.

Jesus, I know that I have sinned against You and violated your holy standards. I confess my sin of (name the particular sin). Today, I ask You to forgive me and cleanse me completely from this sin. Thank You that when You forgive me, You choose to remember my sin no more. (Heb. 8:12; 10:17) *You remove my sins as far away as the east is from the west* (Ps. 103:12) *and bury them in the depths of the sea.* (Mic. 7:19) *Thank You, Jesus, for forgiving me, and I also choose to forgive myself.*

I ask this in Your name. Amen

Dealing with the Enemy

The Bible is clear that we have an enemy. His name is Satan and he has many fallen angels, known as demons that work for him. They hate God and they hate humans because we are created in God's image. They especially hate Christians. They will do all they can to hurt us and damage our relationships, especially our relationship with God. Attacking marriages and families is one of their most common strategies because God designed both. They want to damage them and even destroy them in any way possible.

From here on, I will simply refer to Satan and his demons as the enemy. The enemy tries to get a hold in our lives in any way possible. Sometimes, the enemy builds a stronghold in our lives if we allow him to do so. Sometimes, he may just have his foot in the door, so to speak, in some small area. I refer to any area the enemy has a hold in our lives as "enemy attachments." These are specific areas the enemy is attached to our lives. Many times, these enemy attachments are generational in families. For instance, if you struggle with anger, your father was angry and your grandfather was angry, then it is likely there is a generational enemy of anger in your family. Not all enemy attachments are generational. We can pick up an enemy attachment in other ways, a few examples are exposure to the occult, drug use, rebellion and exposure to pornography.

Here are some of the most common enemy attachments: pornography, drug addiction, alcoholism, anger, depression, rejection, pride, fear, and anxiety. There can be many others. The way we find out whether we have any enemy attachments is by asking Jesus. Of course, He knows and will reveal them to us if we simply ask Him. He will also free us from any enemy when we ask Him to do so.

Below is a prayer for dealing with enemy attachments. If you struggle with any of the enemy attachments listed above or know of any other area where you don't seem able to get the victory, pray this prayer for those specific areas.

Jesus, You know that I struggle with (area of struggle). Please, show me if there is an enemy attachment connected to that struggle.

Pause and listen for Jesus to speak to your heart. If there is an enemy attachment in the area Jesus will confirm that to you. If He tells you there is, then continue this prayer. If Jesus tells you there isn't, you don't need to continue this prayer. Instead go back and pray about the next area of struggle.

Jesus, please command the enemy of (area of struggle) to leave. Judge him and send him where You want him sent. Forbid him to return. Put a hedge of protection around my mind, my heart, my soul, my body, my life and my relationship with (your spouse). Thank You for the victory I have in Your blood. Jesus, what do You want to put in my life in place of (area of struggle)?

Pause and let Jesus speak to your heart.

After you have prayed this prayer for every area of struggle of which you are aware, pray the following prayer.

Jesus, please, show me if there are any other enemy attachments in my life.

Pause and let Jesus speak to your heart. If Jesus brings anything to your mind, pray the above prayer, asking Jesus to remove that enemy. When Jesus doesn't bring anything else to your mind, pray the following prayer.

Jesus, if I am clean of all enemy attachments, please, prompt clean.

Pause and let Jesus speak to your heart. If there are no more enemy attachments, Jesus will confirm that you are clean of all enemies. If He does not do that, return to the previous prayer and ask Jesus to reveal any other enemy attachments. Continue this until Jesus confirms you are clean from all enemies.

This is a lot with which to deal. The three areas of emotional pain, sin, and enemy attachments are heavy loads to carry in our backpacks. That is why it is vital that we deal with these areas. Only after these weights are removed can we take off the backpacks that damage our marriages. With our heavy packs gone, we can enjoy the marriage that God intends for us. The following chapters will deal with how to build that kind of fulfilling relationship.

Review:

1. In the section "Acknowledge the Pain":

   • Did you find this section helpful? _____ Why or why not?

   _____

   _____

   _____

   _____

   • Did it help you understand yourself better?_____
   If so, what was one area that you now understand yourself better?

   _____

   _____

_____

_____

2. In the section "Releasing the Pain":

    • Did you find this section helpful? _____ Why or why not?

    _____

    _____

    _____

    _____

3. In the Section "Dealing with Sin":

    • Did you find this section helpful? _____ Why or why not?

    _____

    _____

    _____

    _____

    • How do you think sin can affect a marriage relationship?

    _____

    _____

    _____

    _____

- Have you ever experienced sin's effect in your own marriage?

_____

If so, how?

_____

_____

_____

4. In the section "Dealing with the Enemy":

- As you prayed, did Jesus reveal any enemy attachments to you?

_____

If so, what were they?

_____

_____

_____

_____

- How did this/these enemy attachment(s) affect your marriage?

_____

_____

_____

_____

Prayer Time:

Theme Thought: I need to deal with my emotional pain, sin and enemy issues in order to experience God's plan for my marriage.

- Thank Jesus for caring about your emotional pain.
- Thank Him for revealing and forgiving your sin.
- Thank Him for revealing and removing enemy attachments in your life. Thank Him for the victory you have in His blood.
- Ask Jesus to show you any way that your emotional pain from your past has damaged your marriage relationship.
- Ask Jesus to help you to respond differently in the future.
- Ask Jesus to help you to be sensitive to the Holy Spirit in the future so that you can quickly recognize and confess any sin.
- Also, ask Jesus to help you to be sensitive to the Holy Spirit in order to quickly recognize and respond to any attack from the enemy

7

THE PAST IMPACTS THE PRESENT

Those that fail to learn from history, are doomed to repeat it.

Winston Churchill

Most couples get married thinking they are making a fresh start, which they are. However, that doesn't mean that everything that happened to them or that they did before marriage just magically disappears. In the last chapter, we discussed the importance of dealing with emotional pain, confessing sin and renouncing enemy attachments in our lives. In this chapter, we want to specifically address past relationships and related issues. Unless these issues and relationships are dealt with correctly, they can continue to affect your marriage relationship.

Dealing with Abuse

Any kind of abuse in your past will impact your marriage, especially if you have experienced sexual abuse. A sexual relationship between a husband and wife is to be a wonderful, mutually enjoyable part of the marriage relationship. That was God's intent in designing sex and marriage. However, a person who has experienced sexual abuse will have a very difficult time enjoying that physical part of his or her marriage unless he or she has worked through and resolved that abuse.

A person who has been the victim of sexual abuse may feel controlled, that he/she can't trust anyone, dirty, defenseless, guilty, pressured, ruined, scared, scarred, shamed, trapped, trashed, violated and wounded. These are just a few of the emotions an abused person may experience.

When that person gets married those feelings will continue. Every time his/her spouse wants to have sex, the abused person will again feel those emotions. A sexual relationship in marriage is not wrong. However, because the person was damaged sexually in the past; it prevents him/her from enjoying a proper physical relationship with his/her spouse now.

The good news is, the past abuse can be resolved and Jesus can take away that person's pain. Below is a chart to help you to identify any abuse and emotional pain you might have experienced. See the example.

Name:	How this person made me feel:
my cousin	*he touched me inappropriately*

Now, in the following chart, identify the emotional pain that the abuse caused. If you aren't sure, take some time to talk to Jesus. Ask Him to show you how that abuse damaged your heart. Ask Him to show you what emotions it caused.

Name:	How this person's abuse made me feel:
my cousin	*confused, controlled, ashamed, dirty*

Now that you have identified abuse from your past, I want to help you resolve the pain from that abuse. The way that we do that is through prayer. By talking to Jesus about what happened and releasing the pain to Him, He can bring healing to your heart. Below is a prayer to help you. Pray this prayer for each person who abused you.

Jesus, You know that (name of person) damaged me by (how this person abused you). That abuse from (name of person) made me feel (how that abuse made you feel).

Jesus, please show me how that abuse damaged my heart.

Pause and listen for Jesus to speak to your heart.

Jesus, how did You feel when (name of person) abused me?

Pause and listen for Jesus to speak to your heart.

Jesus, can You heal my heart from the damage (name of person)'s abuse caused?

Pause and listen for Jesus to speak to your heart.

Jesus, what lies from the enemy did I believe because of this abuse?

Pause and listen for Jesus to speak to your heart.

Jesus, today I want the healing that only You can bring to my heart. You know the pain I have carried because of what (name of person) did to me. I don't want to hold onto that pain any longer. Today, I want to place that pain in Your hands and let it go. Jesus, I don't want to believe those lies from the enemy any longer. Today, I also want to give You those lies and release them.

Jesus, what do you want to put in my life in place of that pain?

Pause and listen for Jesus to speak to your heart.

Jesus, what truth(s) do You want to put in my mind in place of those lies?

Pause and listen for Jesus to speak to your heart.

Jesus, do I need to forgive (name of person) or have I already done that?

Pause and listen for Jesus to speak to your heart. If Jesus indicates that you need to forgive this person continue this prayer of forgiveness. If not, skip to the next section.

Jesus, today I ask You to help me forgive (name of person). I ask You to grant him/her grace, mercy and pardon just as You have me. I am willing to take Your grace to fully forgive and release (name of person). I ask You to turn any consequences of his/her actions into blessings for Your glory and for good in my life. I ask You, Jesus, to take back any ground I gave to the enemy through my unforgiveness and bitterness. I yield that ground to your control.

Jesus, I ask You to separate my mind, heart, soul, body and spirit from (name of person). If there is anything from (name of person) that is still affecting me, please remove it. Anything that was stolen from me by (name of person), please return those things to me. Heal my heart from (name of person) and make me whole again.

Jesus, thank for the healing You have brought to my heart and life today.

Amen.

Dealing with Past Relationships

Relationships from our past can and often do affect our marriage relationship. When we are in a relationship with another person we develop an emotional attachment to that person. In a sense, we give that person a small part of our heart. Then we may break up with that person and move on; however, that part of our heart remains with that former boyfriend or girlfriend. This is especially true when the couple is involved sexually. God designed sex to be a spiritual and emotional, as well as physical, connection. So, every time a person has a sexual relationship with someone to whom he or she is not married, he/she leaves a part of his/her heart with that person.

It is important to break all ties to any previous relationships and ask Jesus to return that part of your heart. You do this through prayer asking Jesus to break any ties and return any missing parts of your heart. It is important to pray this for each person with whom you had a relationship. It is especially important to pray this for every person with whom you had a sexual relationship.

Start by listing below each person with whom you had an emotional and/or sexual relationship. (If needed, continue writing on a separate sheet of paper.)

Name:	Name:	Name:
_____	_____	_____
_____	_____	_____
_____	_____	_____
_____	_____	_____
_____	_____	_____
_____	_____	_____
_____	_____	_____
_____	_____	_____
_____	_____	_____

Once you have listed each person with whom you had a relationship, pray the following prayer for each one you identified.

Jesus, You know about my relationship with (name of person). I ask You to separate my mind, heart, soul, body and spirit from (name of person). If there is anything from (name of person) that is still affecting me, please remove it. Anything that was taken from me by (name of person) or that I gave away to (name of person), please return those things to me. Heal my heart from my relationship with (name of person) and make me whole again. Please, take back any ground I gave to the enemy through my relationship with (name of person). Thank You, Jesus.

I ask this in Your name. Amen

Dealing with Moral Failure

The term "moral failure" simply means any sexual sin, it is a violation of God's perfect moral law. Sexual sin always damages our relationship with God and our spouse. Moral failure before marriage damages our relationship with our spouse after marriage. Moral failure during marriage also has a devastating effect on a marriage. Dealing with sexual sins, like any sin, involves confession and repentance. Failure in this area of our lives brings such shame and guilt that we often don't want to talk about it not even to God. However, it is essential that we deal with our moral failure. If we don't, it will cause walls in our relationship with God and our spouse.

Moral failure is one of the enemy's most effective tools in damaging relationships, marriages, and families. That is why we often hear of Christian leaders who are involved in sexual sin. It is also why so many men and women in our churches are addicted to pornography. So along with confessing and repenting of any moral failure, we also must deal with any enemy attachments that could be driving that sin.

The first step is acknowledging how you have failed in this area. Read through the following chart and mark each area in which you have ever participated.

Moral Failure
____ Fantasy (emotional attachment toward someone other than a spouse)
____ Lust (sexual desires for another person other than a spouse)
____ Sexting
____ Sexual discussion with someone other than a spouse (in person, online or by phone)
____ Pornography (magazines, video, internet)
____ Masturbation
____ Homosexual/lesbian activity
____ Defrauding (sexual arousal of someone other than a spouse)
____ Premarital sexual activity
____ Adultery
____ Exposing oneself
____ Peeping Tom
____ Sexually harassing another person
____ Willingly committing incest with another person
____ Sexually abusing another person
____ wife swapping

Moral Failure (continued)

___ Raping another person

___ Abortion (had one or more; got a woman pregnant who had an abortion)

___ Bestiality

___ Prostituton

___ Topless/Nude bars

___ Cyber sex/phone sex

___ 900 phone numbers

___ Other: _____

_____

After marking each area of moral failure, pray the following prayer for each area that you marked.

Jesus, I realize that I have violated Your perfect moral standards. Today I want to acknowledge and renounce my sinful involvement in (specific moral failure) and ask You to break that stronghold in my life. I ask You, Lord Jesus to take back ground given to the enemy through my involvement and I yield that ground to Your control.

Jesus, do I have an enemy attachment in the area of (specific moral failure)?

Pause and listen for Jesus to speak to your heart. If there is an enemy attachment in the area Jesus will confirm that to you. If He tells you there is, then continue this prayer. If Jesus tells you there isn't you don't need to continue this prayer. Instead go back and pray about the next area of moral failure.

Jesus, please command the enemy of (specific moral failure) to leave. Judge him and send him where You want him sent. Forbid him to return. Put a hedge of protection around my mind, my heart, my soul, my body, my life and my relationship with (your spouse). Thank You for the victory I have in Your blood. Jesus, what do You want to put in my life in place of (specific moral failure)?

Pause and let Jesus speak to your heart.

After you have prayed this prayer for every item you marked on the Moral Failure charts, continue by praying the following.

Jesus, please, show me if there is any other moral failure that I need to confess.

Pause and let Jesus speak to your heart. If Jesus brings anything to your mind pray the above prayer for that particular area of moral failure. After praying through every moral failure, pray the following prayer.

Jesus, thank You for Your forgiveness and cleansing. Help me to forgive myself for each of these areas of moral failure. If I am tempted in any of these areas, remind me that You are there for me and You want to help me. Help me be quick to run to You and away from temptation. Thank You that You promise that You have forgiven me and You will cleanse me from all unrighteousness.

I ask this in Your name. Amen

To experience the kind of fulfilling marriage relationship that God wants us to have, it is essential that we correctly deal with our past. Often a person will try to move on and forget about the past. However, he or she can't really move on until he/she has resolved past abuse, relationships and/or moral sin. Only after resolving those issues can each of us enjoy marriage as God designed it.

Dealing with moral failure is especially difficult. In our counseling office, we lead every person through this same process of confessing and asking God's forgiveness for their various moral sins. Then when we are finished, we have them take that sheet listing all their moral failures and feed it through our paper shredder. We do this as a visual illustration that God forgives us completely when we confess these sins. God obviously never forgets anything; however, He chooses to remember our sins no more when we confess them. (Hebrews 8:12; 10:17) Also, Scripture tells us that He removes our sin as far as the east is from the west. (Psalm 103:12) It also says that God casts our sins in the depths of the sea. Since God can and does forgive us, it is important that we also forgive ourselves. Sexual sins bring guilt and shame; however, after we confess them God forgives and cleanses us. He wants us to experience His peace and joy. The enemy wants us to focus on our past failures. God wants us to walk in freedom and experience His wonderful plans for us.

Review:

1. In the section "Dealing with Abuse":

    *   How do you think sexual abuse in the past could affect a person's marriage relationship?

        _____

        _____

        _____

        _____

    *   Have you experienced this yourself? _____ How was your marriage affected?

        _____

        _____

        _____

        _____

    *   If you experienced sexual abuse, how did God bring healing to your heart as you worked through this chapter?

        _____

        _____

        _____

        _____

2. In the section "Dealing with Past Relationships":

   • Did you find this section helpful? _____ Why or why not?

   _____

   _____

   _____

   _____

   • Have past relationships affected your marriage in any way? _____ If so how?

   _____

   _____

   _____

   _____

3. In the section "Dealing with Moral Failure":

   • Did you find this section helpful? _____ Why or why not?

   _____

   _____

   _____

   _____

- How do you think past moral failure could affect a couple's present marriage relationship?

  _____

  _____

  _____

  _____

- Has your marriage ever been affected by moral failure, either yours, your spouse's or both? _____ If so, how was your marriage affected?

  _____

  _____

  _____

  _____

4. Have you ever struggled with not being able to forgive yourself for your failures even though you confessed them and asked God to forgive you? _____

   Why do you think the enemy wants us to continue to focus on our past sins and failures?

   _____

   _____

   _____

   _____

Prayer Time:

Theme Thought: I need to deal with any abuse, relationships and moral failure in my past.

- Thank Jesus for caring about your pain, even the pain of abuse.
- Thank Jesus for healing your heart from any past relationships.
- Thank Jesus for forgiving your moral failure.
- Ask Jesus to show you any way that abuse from your past has affected your relationship with your spouse.
- Ask Jesus to help you to respond differently in the future.
- Ask Jesus to show you if past relationships have affected the way you respond to your spouse.
- Ask Jesus to help you to respond differently in the future.
- Ask Jesus to show you any way that your moral failure has damaged your marriage relationship.
- Ask Jesus to help you to love your spouse unselfishly.

8

The "F" and "P" Words in Marriage

A happy marriage is the union of two good forgivers.

Ruth Bell Graham

You did not marry a perfect person. Your spouse did not marry a perfect person. I'm sure those two true statements did not surprise you. Whether you have been married a year or fifty years, you know that your spouse has failings and shortcomings, just like you do. Adam and Eve were the only ones to experience marriage to a sinless person and even they didn't experience it very long.

Even as Christians, we still sin and make mistakes. We make unwise choices which hurt others. This is especially true in marriage. Marriage is the closest relationship we will ever experience on earth. With marriage comes an openness and vulnerability, which is essential to enjoy the oneness God designed for marriage. However, since we are each married to an imperfect sinner, our spouse can also hurt us worse than anyone else. In this fallen world, it is inevitable that each of us hurts our spouse and our spouse hurts us. Usually, it isn't intentional but it still happens and it still hurts. Often our most painful wounds come from the one we love the most.

My wife Wendy and I love to do premarital counseling with engaged couples. They are fun. They are in love anticipating their upcoming marriage. Usually, they don't have walls in their relationship yet. They can hardly take their eyes off each other.

I turn to the young man and say, "I hate to break this to you, but you are not marrying a perfect woman."

Then I'll look at the young lady and say, "I'm sorry but you're not marrying a perfect man."

"There will come a day when your husband or wife is going to say or do something that hurts you. It may not happen until after you've been married a month or a few months. It might happen on your Honeymoon. I don't know when it will happen, but it will happen. The best thing you can do for your marriage is to determine right now that when it happens you will forgive him or her. Forgiveness will help you build a strong marriage that will last a lifetime. Unforgiveness will destroy your marriage, your relationship, and your family. If you want to be a good husband or wife, decide today to be a good forgiver."

We have seen marriages destroyed by unforgiveness and bitterness. We have also seen husbands and wives forgive their respective spouses for horrendous transgressions. Those marriages are stronger today than ever before. Forgiveness is important if we want to enjoy the fulfilling marriage relationship God wants us to enjoy.

Christ-like Forgiveness

How does God want me to forgive my spouse? Jesus is our perfect example. He is the perfect Forgiver. When Jesus was on earth, He was eager to forgive. He forgave a paralyzed man before the man asked in response to his faith. (Matthew 9; Mark 2; Luke 5) Jesus forgave a woman with a terrible reputation. (Luke 7:36-47) As Jesus hung on the cross dying, He forgave those that put Him there. (Luke 23:34) Jesus is still eager to forgive us today. (Psalm 86:5) That's why He encourages us to confess our sins and accept His forgiveness. (I John 1:7-9) Jesus Christ's forgiveness flows out of His great sacrificial love for us. (Colossians 1:13,14)

Jesus can help you to forgive your spouse regardless of how badly he or she has hurt you. There is nothing your spouse can say or do that is so bad that Jesus can't help you to forgive him or her.

One time we counseled a couple that was extremely antagonistic to each other. They had both hurt each other greatly. The first day in our office they wouldn't look at each other or talk to each other. Later that week, I prayed with the husband. He wept as Jesus showed him how his anger and moral failure had damaged his wife. When we finished praying, the husband with tears in his eyes turned to his wife and asked her to forgive him.

The wife looked her husband in the eye and said, "I wish I could... but I can't."

The next day, Wendy prayed with the wife. Jesus brought great healing to her heart and told the wife she needed to forgive her husband. She willingly prayed and forgave her husband.

The last day we met with them, this couple was holding hands, looking into each other's eyes and communicating from the heart.

Some of you reading this have been hurt deeply from infidelity and/or abuse. I know that you have been wounded deeply. However, I can say with complete certainty, Jesus can help you to forgive.

Genuine Forgiveness in Marriage

I was blessed to be raised in a Christian home with two younger brothers. Brothers can be extremely irritating. (I assume sisters are the same but I can't say from experience.) There were many times we would upset each other. My parents strongly encouraged us to apologize and forgive each other.

The offender would mumble, "I'm sorry."

The offended would say, "I forgive you" and then add more quietly, "But I won't forget it."

Even as one of us would mouth the words, that one would be plotting his revenge against the other brother. It should be obvious that isn't genuine forgiveness.

There is a lot of misunderstanding when it comes to the area of forgiveness. Forgiveness is not simply saying the words. Forgiveness is not dependent on anything the offender does or doesn't do. Forgiveness doesn't in any way diminish the pain of the offender's words and/or actions. Forgiveness doesn't take away the memory of the offense. Forgiveness isn't denying that we were hurt. What is forgiveness?

When someone hurts you, in a sense, that person sins against you; like when we hurt God we sin against Him. Any time there is sin there is always a price to be paid. There is always a cost involved, such as emotional pain and other consequences. In essence, the offender owes the offended a debt. We sin against God and our sin has a price attached to it. We couldn't pay the debt of our sin. Jesus paid our debt for us at the cross. In the same way, nothing the offender does can "pay" for his or her sin against you. They can apologize and they might make you feel some better. However, it doesn't take away the memory or even the pain of the offense. The only one who can cancel that debt is you, the one who was hurt. You must choose to forgive and release the other person.

You don't forgive because the other person deserves it. You forgive to protect yourself from bitterness. Bitterness is a poison, which will destroy your relationship with God, your spouse, and others. (Acts 8:22, 23) That is why God encourages all of us to put away all bitterness and be quick to forgive the same way He forgives us. (Ephesians 4:31, 32)

Forgiveness is an important tool for every marriage. If you want to enjoy the best marriage possible, learner to be a good forgiver. Also, learn to recognize when you have hurt your spouse and be quick to ask him or her to forgive you.

Forgiving my Spouse

Start by identifying each way that your spouse has hurt you. On the following chart, list each way you have been hurt and how each hurt made you feel. Only list the hurts for which you have not already genuinely forgiven him/her. (Continue on additional paper if necessary.)

Ways My Spouse Has Hurt Me:	How It Made Me Feel:
_____	_____
_____	_____
_____	_____
_____	_____
_____	_____
_____	_____
_____	_____
_____	_____
_____	_____

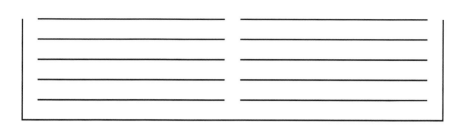

Then pray the following prayer for each hurt on your list.

Jesus, you know that (spouse's name) has hurt me by (specific hurt from spouse) causing me to feel (specific feelings). Jesus, what did that do to my heart?

Pause and let Jesus speak to your heart.

Jesus, can you heal my heart from that pain?

Pause and let Jesus speak to your heart.

Jesus, I don't want to hold on to this pain any longer. It's too heavy and it hurts too much. Today I want to place this pain in your hands and let it go.

Jesus, I acknowledge that (spouse's name) has sinned against me by (specific hurt from spouse) causing me to feel (specific feelings). I ask that You grant (spouse's name) grace, mercy and pardon just as You have me. Today I am willing to take Your grace to cancel the debt (spouse's name) owes me because of his/her (specific hurt from spouse). I ask you to turn any consequences into blessings for your glory and for good in my life. I ask You, Lord, to take back any ground I gave to the enemy through my unforgiveness and bitterness. I yield that ground to Your control.

After praying the above prayer for each hurt on your list, pray the following prayer.

Jesus, is there any other way that (spouse's name) hurt me for which I have not forgiven him/her?

Pause and listen for Jesus to speak to your heart. If He brings anything else to your mind, pray the above prayer for each thing that Jesus brings to mind. When He doesn't bring anything else to mind pray the following prayer.

Jesus, thank You for healing my heart and helping me to forgive (spouse's name). I know that there will be times that (spouse's name) will hurt me again. When that happens, remind me to come to You. You will heal my heart and You will help me to forgive (spouse's name). Thank You for my spouse. He (or she) is a special gift from You. Help me to remember that every day.

I ask this in Your name. Amen

Identifying How I Hurt My Spouse

Next, it is important to identify each way that you have hurt your spouse. It may be difficult for you to really understand how you have hurt your spouse. However, Jesus knows every way that you have hurt your husband/wife. So you will begin this section with the following prayer.

Jesus, You know my every word and action. You know that some of my words and/or actions have damaged my spouse. Please, show me every way that I have hurt (spouse's name).

Pause and listen for Jesus to speak to your heart. List each thing that Jesus has shown you in the following chart.

Jesus, please show me how each of these hurtful words or actions damaged my husband's/wife's heart. What emotional pain did they cause my (spouse's name)?

Pause and listen for Jesus to speak to your heart. List the emotional pain next to each area of hurt.

Ways I Hurt My Spouse:	How It Made My Spouse Feel:

```
_____     _____
_____     _____
_____     _____
_____     _____
_____     _____
_____     _____
_____     _____
```

After listing all the hurts of which you are aware, pray the following prayer for each item on the list.

Jesus, You know that I have hurt (spouse's name) by my (specific hurt I caused my spouse). I understand that my (specific hurt I caused my spouse) caused (spouse's name) to feel (specific feelings). Today I take responsibility for my actions and I ask You to forgive me for hurting the husband/wife that You gave me. By sinning against (spouse's name), I also sinned against You. I humbly ask You to forgive me and help me not to hurt (spouse's name) by my (specific hurt I caused my spouse) in the future. Give me the courage to ask (spouse's name) to forgive me for hurting him (or her) in this way.

After praying through this chart, arrange a time when you can sit down with your spouse and talk. This should be a quiet time away from distractions when you can focus on each other. During that time, ask your spouse to forgive you for each area of hurt you listed on your chart. Use the following as a guide, but use your own words.

I know that I have hurt you and I am sorry. Today, I am taking responsibility for my hurtful words and actions. I was wrong in (specific hurt I caused my spouse) and I made you feel (specific feelings). I don't want to hurt you again by (specific hurt I caused my spouse). I don't want to cause you to feel (specific feelings). Would you be willing to choose to forgive me today?

Forgiveness is an essential ingredient in every successful marriage. We have counseled hundreds of couples over the years. We praise the Lord that the majority of those couples are still doing well today. However, some of the couples with whom we worked have gotten divorced since meeting with us. One of the key issues leading to each of their divorces was an unwillingness to forgive. Being quick to forgive and ask forgiveness will help to safeguard your marriage against bitterness, which could ultimately destroy your relationship.

Dealing with Pride

Pride goes before destruction, And a haughty spirit before a fall. (Prov. 16:18)

A man's pride will bring him low, But the humble in spirit will retain honor. (Prov. 29:23)

Another area that will damage our relationship with God and our relationship with our spouse is the area of pride. Pride was the original sin. Satan desired to be God. (Isaiah 14:12-15) Pride is still one of the enemy's favorite tools to damage our relationships with God and each other.

To enjoy the marriage relationship with your spouse that God wants the two of you to enjoy, you will both need God's help. Pride creates a wall in our relationship with our Heavenly Father. Pride will also damage a marriage. No one enjoys being married to a proud person. So, it is essential that you deal with any pride in your life.

Read through the following charts. Mark each statement which you feel if true about yourself.

Identifying Pride
_____ I tend to focus on myself.
_____ I tend to focus on the failures of others.
_____ I tend to get hurt feelings if someone else is promoted instead of me.
_____ I tend to be critical of others and am quick to notice their faults.
_____ I desire to be appreciated by others.
_____ I desire to be recognized for my accomplishments.
_____ I tend to draw attention to my abilities and/or achievements.
_____ I tend to feel sorry for myself when others don't appreciate me.
_____ I tend to be independent and self-sufficient.

_____ I feel the need to prove when I'm right.

_____ I tend to be defensive when someone criticizes or corrects me.

_____ I feel it important to claim my rights.

_____ I enjoy when others serve me.

_____ I desire to be successful without seeking God's guidance.

_____ I enjoy self-advancement.

_____ I am very concerned with what others think of me.

_____ I want people to recognize that I am important to my family, job, church, etc.

_____ I am very confident in my knowledge and understanding.

Identifying Pride (continued)

_____ I am self-conscious fearing that others my think my think badly of me.

_____ I am quick to blame others when something goes wrong.

_____ I tend to look down on others, thinking they are lower than myself.

_____ My reputation and public image is very important to me.

_____ I tend to cover up my sin. I don't want anyone else to know.

_____ I find it difficult to share my struggles or ask others to pray for me.

Now that you have identified each area of pride in your life, pray the following prayer for each area of pride that you marked.

Jesus, I know that I have sinned against You with my pride. Today I want to acknowledge and renounce each area of pride in my life. I confess that (specific area of pride). I choose to humble myself and response with a humble attitude.

After praying through each area of pride that you marked on the chart, pray the following prayer.

Jesus, I want to be free from all pride in my life. Please, show me if there is any other pride in my life.

Pause and listen for Jesus to speak to your heart. If Jesus brings any other area(s) of pride to your mind pray the above prayer for each area of pride. After confessing all areas of pride, finish by praying the following prayer.

Jesus, thank You for forgiving my pride. I want to be humble so that I can experience Your grace. I choose to submit to You and to the leadership You have placed in my life. Take back any ground I gave to the enemy through my pride in these areas. I yield that ground to Your control. Jesus, what do You want to put in my heart and life in place of my pride?

Pause and listen for Jesus to speak to your heart. Write what Jesus tells you below.

Jesus wants to replace my pride with:

_____

_____

Both forgiveness and humility are important to a successful marriage the way God designed it. Both husband and wife need to be quick to forgive. Each also needs to humbly put the needs of his or her spouse before himself or herself. That is what God intends for every marriage.

Review:

1. In the section "Christ-like Forgiveness":

    *   When Jesus was on earth, what are some ways He modelled forgiveness?

_____

_____

_____

_____

- What are some ways Jesus exemplifies forgiveness now?

_____

_____

_____

_____

- What can we learn from Jesus about forgiveness?

_____

_____

_____

_____

2. In the section "Genuine Forgiveness in Marriage":

- How would you define genuine forgiveness?

_____

_____

_____

_____

- Before working through this chapter, who in the past has shown you genuine forgiveness?

_____

_____

_____

_____

- How did it feel to be forgiven?

_____

_____

_____

_____

3. In the section "Identifying How I Hurt My Spouse":

    - How did you feel after praying, releasing the pain and forgiving your spouse?

_____

_____

_____

_____

4. In the section "Identifying How I Hurt My Spouse":

    - How did you feel after you prayed and then asked your spouse to forgive you?

_____

_____

_____

_____

5. In the section "Dealing with Pride":

  • Did you find this section helpful? _____ Why or why not?

  _____

  _____

  _____

  _____

  • Have you ever experienced pride affecting your marriage?

  _____

  If so, how?

  _____

  _____

  _____

  _____

  • How did you feel after you prayed through your pride?

  _____

  _____

  _____

  _____

- What are some negative ways you think pride could affect a marriage?

_____

_____

_____

_____

Prayer Time:

Theme Thought: I need to deal with hurts in my marriage and my pride.

- Thank Jesus for His forgiveness.
- Thank Jesus for caring about the pain caused by your spouse.
- Thank Jesus for giving you the courage to seek forgiveness from your spouse.
- Ask Jesus to show you the ways you have responded to pain from your spouse.
- Ask Jesus to help you to respond differently in the future.

- Ask Jesus to help you be quick to forgive your spouse when he/she does hurt you.
- Ask Jesus to show you how your spouse has responded to pain caused by you.
- Ask Jesus to help you not to hurt your spouse in the future.
- Ask Jesus to show you how pride has damaged your relationship with your spouse.
- Ask Jesus to help you respond humbly to your spouse in the future.
- Ask Jesus to help you be sensitive to the Holy Spirit so you can quickly identify and confess any pride in the future.

9

PREPARING FOR HEART-FOCUSED COMMUNICATION

Keep your heart with all diligence, for out of it spring the issues of life.

King Solomon (Prov. 4:23)

Most of us probably played the game *Gossip* when we were children. It is the game where a number of people sit in a circle. One person whispers something to the person next to him or her. Then, that person whispers it to the next person, and so on until the whispered sentence goes all the way around the circle. Usually, the sentence the last person hears is much different than the original sentence. This doesn't just happen in kid's games. Miscommunication often happens in marriage.

We ask every couple with whom we meet, "What would you like to accomplish in counseling?" The answer that we hear the most is, "We want to learn to communicate better."

Communication between a husband and wife always involves four elements:

1. What the person intends to say
2. What the person actually says
3. What the spouse hears
4. What the spouse thinks he/she heard

Often, numbers 1 and 4 are completely different. Just like the game Gossip, what the first person intended and what the second person thinks he (or she) heard can be vastly different. We can actually extrapolate this concept even farther by adding two more elements. Before number 1, we could add "The emotions behind what the person intends to say". Then after number 4, we could also add "The emotions the spouse thinks are behind what he (or she) thinks he (or she) heard". Obviously, those two can be even farther apart. This is one of the reasons that so many couples struggle with communication. We often make assumptions about what our respective spouses mean that are often wrong. We all do it at times.

How can we prevent these misunderstandings? Heart-focused communication can help to keep these misunderstandings from happening. Every husband has to be able to focus on his wife's heart and every wife has to be able to focus on her husband's heart. Communicating on the heart level will help to prevent assumptions, which lead to misunderstandings.

But how do we do that?

We often get married thinking this "marriage thing" will be easy, especially Christian marriage. At least that's what I did. I read several popular marriage books by Christian authors. At the small Bible College where my wife and I met, we even took a course called *Preparation for Family Living*. So, when we got married, I thought I wouldn't have any problem mastering marriage. All I had to do was apply those principles I had learned and life would be perfect. The things we had learned were helpful, but we still had problems sometimes. I would say something, and Wendy would think I was saying something completely different than what I meant. Then, I would try to explain why what she was thinking was wrong, which made things worse. She would begin to cry and ask me to stop lecturing her. Then, I really didn't know what to do. I would either try harder to explain why she shouldn't be upset or just pull away and not say anything at all. Both responses only made things worse.

There were also times when Wendy would say something and I assumed that she was upset or that I had failed to live up to her expectations in some way. Then, I would get angry and start to defend myself, or I would get driven and try to do more to make her happy. Either of these responses, of course, hurt Wendy. Then, she might say or do something that hurt me. I would reciprocate by saying or doing something that hurt her.

Right now, some of you are nodding your heads. You have been on that same merry-go-round. It isn't fun, is it? We would get stuck in that *Vicious Cycle,* and we didn't know how to get out. We will talk more about the Vicious Cycle later in this chapter. For now, just understand that every couple has their own cycle. Often, miscommunication helps to start that Vicious Cycle spinning.

Almost none of us get married knowing how to connect with our spouse's heart. We know how to communicate intellectually, but not on a heart level. Wendy and I didn't learn heart-focused communication until we had been married 25 years. However, it was one of the best things we ever did for our marriage.

As I said before, Wendy and I love to counsel engaged couples or even pre-engaged couples. Pre-marital counseling is our favorite kind of counseling. Usually, a pre-marital couple doesn't have walls in their relationship. They are usually eager to learn to care for each other and communicate on a heart level. It's always fun to lead them through this process. By teaching them to do this before they are married, we are giving them a useful tool to help them build a strong, successful marriage.

The good news is that any couple can learn heart-focused communication if they are willing to do so. Any couple can learn to connect from the heart.

The first necessity in establishing a heart connection is dealing with our baggage from the past. That's why the last three chapters dealt with experiencing healing for past pain, as well as confessing moral failure and pride. That's why I also led you through the process of forgiving your spouse. All of these can cause walls in your relationship with your spouse. They can keep you from being able to open your heart to your spouse completely, which is essential to connect with to his (or her) heart.

Before you go on, take some time and go back over the last three chapters. Ask Jesus to show you if there is any other pain with which you haven't dealt or any sin that you haven't confessed. When you are sure that you have worked through each of those areas thoroughly, proceed to the next section.

Identifying Pain Buttons

We all have *Pain Buttons.* These are specific areas of emotional pain from our past. When we get married our Pain Buttons are already in place.

It is only a matter of time until our respective spouses step on one or more of our Pain Buttons and we step on theirs. It is important to identify each Pain Button or category of pain, to better understand ourselves and our spouses. This will help you avoid hurting your spouse and help him (or her) avoid hurting you.

Below are common Pain Buttons (categories of pain). Look back at chapter 7 and review the ways you were hurt and feelings associated with each hurt. Also, look at chapter 8 and review the section on Sexual Abuse.

The following list contains some common Pain Buttons. Next to each one are some emotional pain words or phrases, which are often associated with that particular Pain Button. Place a number **1** by the Pain Button that is most painful for you, a number **2** by the second and so on. Put a **0** by those where you don't feel any pain.

Pain Buttons:

_____ Alone – abandoned, didn't belong, excluded, lonely, left out, neglected, rejected, unloved, unnoticed, unwanted

_____ Not a Priority – desires rejected, insignificant, misunderstood, not important, not listened to, not valued

_____ Controlled/Taken Advantage Of – conspired against, deceived, defeated, disrespected, dominated, helpless, manipulated, pressured, tricked

_____ Sexual Abuse – can't trust anyone, cheated, dirty, exposed, guilty, molested, ruined, trapped, unsafe, violated, vulnerable

_____ Failed Expectations – always wrong, can't do anything right, don't measure up, failure, not good enough, pressured to perform

_____ Put Down – belittled, blamed, despised, hated, made fun of, judged, mocked, picked on, shamed, ridiculed

_____ Blame Myself – all my fault, I should know better, I should do better, if I were only better, hate myself

_____ Anxiety/Depression – afraid, angry, anxious, discouraged, disappointed, fearful, empty, frightened, sad, scared, suicidal

If you have trouble identifying your Pain Buttons, spend some time talking to Jesus. Ask Him to show you in which of these areas you struggle.

Identifying Pain Responses

We all have emotional pain. We also all respond to that pain in some way. Usually, our natural responses are emotionally, spiritually and relationally unhealthy. When we are married, those responses often hurt our spouses and damage our marriages. That is why it is important to identify our response patterns.

How do you respond when someone hurts you and/or you are struggling emotionally?

Read through the following list. Circle every response that you have ever done. Then, look at all those you circled. Choose the top three that you do most often. Decide which of the three you do most often and write a number **1** on the line in front of that response. Decide which of the remaining two responses that you do the most and write a number **2** on the line in front of it. Write the number **3** in front of the remaining response.

Pain Responses

_____ Detach Emotionally – shut my emotions down so I don't feel

_____ Check Out Mentally – think about something else

_____ Disassociate – my mind goes elsewhere and I don't remember it later

_____ Disengage – pull away emotionally

_____ Distance – walk away from the person who is hurting me

_____ Freeze – don't know what to say or do, can't respond

_____ Self-Focus – all I can think about is myself and my pain

_____ Dominate – try to control others to protect myself

_____ Critical – criticize and find fault in others to protect myself

_____ Anger – feel very frustrated and angry, possibly demonstrated in words/actions

_____ Addictions – go into pornography, alcohol, drugs, internet, food, gambling, etc.

_____ Rebellion – respond with defiance refusing to give in

_____ Driven – throw myself into work, stay busy to protect myself

_____ Dishonesty – lie or tell "half-truths" to protect myself

_____ Silence – stop talking

_____ Talk – talk constantly

_____ Joke – clown around and laugh

Identifying Your Vicious Cycle

Now that you have identified your Pain Buttons and Pain Responses, we can begin putting the pieces together. In section **A** on the chart below, list your top three Pain Buttons. In section **B** list you top three Pain Responses.

A (Pain Buttons)

1. _____
2. _____
3. _____

B (Pain Responses)

1. _____
2. _____
3. _____

You have now identified your half of your Vicious Cycle. When someone steps on one or more of your Pain Buttons (Section **A**), you respond with one or more of your Pain Responses (Section **B**). It is important to identify your half of the Vicious Cycle first. Now, you and your spouse need to work together to identify the Vicious Cycle in your marriage.

On the next page, there is a diagram of the complete cycle. Working with your spouse, fill in the blanks together. Write the husband's Pain Buttons in section **A** on the chart. Then, write the husband's Pain Responses in Section **B** on the chart. Write the wife's Pain Buttons in section **C** and her Pain Responses in section **D**.

You have now identified your marriage's Vicious Cycle.

Let me give you an example of how Wendy and I have experienced the Vicious Cycle in our marriage. One of my Pain Buttons is *Failed Expectations*. There have been times when I felt I wasn't living up to expectations, whether they were expectations at work, church, home or simply expectations I put on myself. I would respond by becoming more driven. I would throw myself into doing more at work, church, home or all three. One of Wendy's Pain Buttons is feeling alone. So the busier I became, the less time I would spend with her. This made her feel all alone. She would feel like I didn't really love her. In response, she might go silent or disengage. Then, I sense that something is wrong. I would think that I was failing her expectations even more, so I work even harder. This makes Wendy feel more alone, so she disengages even more. In turn, I feel like I'm failing her even more and get more driven. Then, she feels more alone and pulls away even more. You get the idea. The Vicious Cycle would just keep going.

This happens to every couple. Every couple has its own Vicious Cycle. You have just identified yours on the chart below.

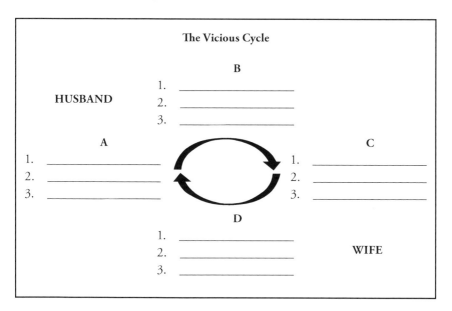

The Vicious Cycle

B

HUSBAND
1. _____
2. _____
3. _____

A
1. _____
2. _____
3. _____

C
1. _____
2. _____
3. _____

D
1. _____
2. _____
3. _____

WIFE

Before we can discuss heart-focused communication, it is important for each of us to identify and understand the Vicious Cycle of our respective marriages. Poor communicate or hurtful words can start the Vicious Cycle whirling. That is why we have taken the time to identify this cycle first.

Understanding the Vicious Cycle in your marriage will help you understand what is really happening every time you and your spouse have a conflict. You are inadvertently stepping on each other's Pain Buttons. Then, you are both responding to that pain in ways that cause more pain for each other.

The good news is there is a better way to respond to each other. There is a better way to communicate, which doesn't trip the Vicious Cycle. The alternative to the Vicious Cycle is called the *Caring Cycle* and it is responding to each other the way God always intended. The alternative to poor communication is heart-focused communication. We are going to talk much more about these in the chapters to come.

Review:

1. Think about an instance of miscommunication or poor communication in your marriage.

    - What were the circumstances surrounding the miscommunication?

    _____

    _____

    _____

    _____

    - What did you think your spouse was saying?

    _____

    _____

    _____

    _____

    - What did your spouse think you were saying?

    _____

    _____

    _____

    _____

- How did you resolve this misunderstanding?

_____

_____

_____

_____

2. Think about your Vicious Cycle.

- What are some ways your spouse has step on your pain buttons during your marriage?

_____

_____

_____

_____

- What are some ways you stepped on your spouse's pain buttons?

_____

_____

_____

_____

- How have you seen your responses to pain cause pain for your spouse?

_____

_____

_____

_____

- How have you experienced your spouse's responses to pain causing you pain?

_____

_____

_____

_____

- When was the first time in your relationship that you can remember the Vicious Cycle happening? What were the circumstances?

_____

_____

_____

_____

We have been talking about some of the ways you and your spouse have experienced the Vicious Cycle in your relationship. In the last chapter, we talked about the importance of forgiveness in your marriage. Before you continue, take some quiet time with Jesus. Ask Jesus to show you if there is anything your spouse has done to step on your pain for which you have not forgiven him/her. Using the forgiveness prayer in the last chapter, forgive your husband/wife for anything that Jesus brings to your mind.

Prayer Time:

Theme Thought: I need to understand how miscommunication damages my marriage. I need to understand my pain and how I respond to it. I also need to understand my spouse's pain and how he/she responds.

- Thank Jesus for caring about your pain.
- Thank Jesus for caring about your spouse's pain.
- Thank Jesus for showing you how you have responded to pain in your marriage.
- Thank Jesus for showing you how your spouse has responded to pain in your marriage.
- Ask Jesus to show you both how your responses to pain have hurt each other.
- Ask Jesus to help both of you to respond differently in the future.
- Ask Jesus to help both of you be quick to forgive when you hurt each other.
- Ask Jesus to help you both to stop the Vicious Cycle when it begins to spin.
- Ask Jesus to help you both communicate clearly and understand each other.
- Ask Jesus to help you to listen well and learn to ask good questions.

10

Heart-focused communication in marriage

In that quietness they were speaking their own language,
with their eyes, with the way they stood, with what they put
into the air about them, each knowing what the other was
saying, and having strength one from the other, for they had
been learning through forty years of being together, and their
minds were one.

Richard Llewellyn, *How Green Was My Valley*

As I told you in the last chapter, we ask every couple what they would like to accomplish in their counseling. One of the most common answers is, "We want to learn to communicate better." Married couples don't know how to communicate well. That is a very broad statement and it is not true of every couple. However, probably the majority of couples would agree that statement is true of their relationship.

In the last chapter, we talked about how miscommunication can damage a relationship. Even worse than miscommunication is evil communication. Many couples have experienced so much pain in their marriage they are stuck in an *evil for evil relationship*. The husband says something hurtful to the wife who says something hurtful in return. The Vicious Cycle begins to spin once again. God's Word warns against such damaging communication.

To sum up, all of you be harmonious, sympathetic, brotherly, kindhearted, and humble in spirit; not returning evil for evil or insult for insult, but giving a blessing instead; for you were called for the very purpose that you might inherit a blessing. (1 Pet. 3:8-9 NASB)

Don't use foul or abusive language. Let everything you say be good and helpful, so that your words will be an encouragement to those who hear them. (Eph. 4:29 NLT)

The vicious cycle is normal. Hurting our spouse when he or she hurts us is normal. Responding with hurtful words when we are hurt is normal. God calls us to something better, something higher, something divinely abnormal.

No one enjoys being misunderstood. No one wants to be accused or blamed. Being attacked with words or put down always damages. No one ever wins a battle of words. Both sides lose, regardless of who has the last word.

No marriage should be a place of damaging words. God designed marriage to be the one place where each spouse feels safe to open his or her heart and freely share his or her thoughts and dreams. The good news is that your marriage can be just such a place. In this chapter, I want to help you to make your marriage a safe place for you and your spouse. I want to help you to learn to connect with your spouse from the heart.

Before we move ahead though, it is important to identify any ways you have been damaged by your spouse's words and any ways that your spouse has been damaged by your words. We do this through prayer.

Pray the following prayer.

Jesus, you know that (spouse's name) and I have not always responded well. You know that there were times that I hurt (spouse's name) with my words. You also know that there were times (spouse's name) hurt me with his (or her words). Jesus, I don't want an evil for evil relationship in my marriage. You don't want that either. Please show me anyway that (spouse's name)'s words have damaged my heart and our relationship.

Pause and let Jesus speak to your heart. Below list each instance of hurt that Jesus brings to your mind:

Ways My Spouse's Words Hurt Me:	How It Made Me Feel:

Then pray the following prayer for each instance of hurtful words on your list.

Jesus, you know that (spouse's name) has hurt me by (specific hurt from spouse's words) causing me to feel (specific feelings). Jesus, I don't want to hold on to this pain any longer. It's too heavy and it hurts too much. Today, I want to place this pain in your hands and let it go.

Jesus, I acknowledge that (spouse's name) has sinned against me by (specific hurt from spouse's words) causing me to feel (specific feelings). I ask that You grant (spouse's name) grace, mercy and pardon just as You have me. Today, I am willing to take Your grace to cancel the debt (spouse's name) owes me because of his/her (specific hurt from spouse's words). I ask you to turn any consequences into blessings for your glory and for good in my life. I ask You, Lord, to take back any ground I gave to the enemy through my unforgiveness and bitterness. I yield that ground to Your control.

Continue by praying the following prayer.

Jesus, you know that I have also hurt (spouse's name) with my words. Jesus, please show me anyway that I have hurt (spouse's name) with my words. Also, show me how my words made him/her feel.

Pause and let Jesus speak to your heart. Below list each instance of hurt that Jesus brings to your mind:

Ways I Hurt My Spouse with Words:	How It Made Him/Her Feel:

_____   _____
_____   _____
_____   _____
_____   _____
_____   _____
_____   _____
_____   _____
_____   _____
_____   _____

Now, pray the following prayer for each way that you hurt your spouse. (Each item on the preceding list)

Jesus, I sinned against (spouse's name) with my words. Specifically, I hurt (spouse's name) by (specific hurt to your spouse by your words) causing him/ her to feel (specific feelings). Jesus, I ask You to forgive me for hurting (spouse's name) in this way, and I ask you to bring healing to his/her heart. Jesus, please set a watch before my mouth so I don't hurt (spouse's name) with my words. Jesus, please give we the courage to ask (spouse's name) to forgive me for hurting him/her with my words.

After praying the above prayer for each item on your list, pray the following prayer.

Jesus, please show me if there is any other way that I have hurt my husband/ wife with my words.

Pause and let Jesus speak to your heart. If Jesus brings anything else to your mind, pray the above prayer for each hurtful thing.

Now, take a few minutes and answer the two questions in the box below.

What attracted you to your spouse? _____

_____

_____

_____

What has been the best part of your relationship/marriage? _____

_____

_____

_____

Together Time: Dealing with Hurt

For the rest of this chapter, as well as most of the remainder of the book, both husband and wife will need to work together.

❖ First, I would encourage each of you to ask your spouse to forgive you for hurting him or her with your words. I will walk you through this. So just relax. Take a deep breath. Turn and face each other.

Husband, ask your wife to forgive you for each item, one at a time, on your list of how you have hurt her. Here is an example, feel free to put it in your own words.

(Wife's name), I know that I have hurt you with my words. I hurt you by (specific hurt to your wife by your words). Can you tell me how that made you feel when I said that?

Allow your wife to share how she felt. Don't react, defend or explain. Just accept her feelings. Remember that her feelings are valid, even though you may not have intended to hurt her. After she is done sharing, continue…

(Wife's name), I did not want to make you feel that way, but I did and I'm taking responsibility for my hurtful words. Will you, please, forgive me for hurting you in that way?

Do this for each area of hurt you identified on your list. If your wife is not able to forgive you, just accept that she is not ready yet. Do not react or pressure her. Simply tell her...

I understand that you are not able to forgive me yet. I accept that. I will continue to pray for you, and I trust God that at the right time He will help you to forgive me. I will wait.

Husband, make sure that you follow through on your promise to pray for your wife.

Wife, now you do the same thing. Go down your list of ways you hurt your husband and one at a time, ask his forgiveness. Here is an example to guide you:

(Husband's name), I know that I have hurt you with my words. I hurt you by (specific hurt to your husband by your words). Can you tell me how that made you feel when I said that?

Allow your husband to share how he felt. Don't react, defend or explain. Just accept his feelings. Remember that his feelings are valid, even though you may not have intended to hurt him. After he is done sharing, continue...

(Husband's name), I did not want to make you feel that way, but I did and I take responsibility for my hurtful words. Will you, please, forgive me for hurting you in that way?

Do this for each area of hurt you identified on your list. If your husband is not able to forgive you, just accept that he is not ready yet. Do not react or pressure him. Simply tell him...

I understand that you are not able to forgive me yet. I accept that. I will continue to pray for you, and I trust God that at the right time He will help you to forgive me. I will wait.

Wife, make sure that you follow through on your promise to pray for your husband.

Only after working through past painful communication are we ready to move ahead to a new, better way of communicating: heart-focused communication.

Together Time: Communicating from the Heart

❖ Before we begin this new adventure, I'm going to ask you to stop and pray. Ask Jesus to help you as you begin to communicate from the heart. Husband, as the spiritual leader of your marriage and your home, I want to ask you to pray. Here is a sample prayer you can use if you wish.

Jesus, (wife's name) and I want to communicate well in our marriage. Would You help us both to feel safe? Help us both be able to open our hearts to each other. Remind us that You are here with us right now. You will help us. Protect us from the enemy, who loves to cause miscommunication and walls in our relationship. We commit our time to You, Lord Jesus.

Amen.

As we continue, I will help you begin to communicate on a heart level. Sometimes, I may refer to the little boy or the little girl. Inside every man there is a little boy, which is actually his heart. That doesn't sound very masculine, so men will often try to hide the little boy inside with manly activities and macho talk. However, if each man would be honest, he would admit that in the depths of his being he still feels like a little boy. The same is true of women. They just tend to use other tactics to try to hide from that little girl inside. A person can hide it, deny it, ignore it, but that doesn't make it any less real. No matter what a person does to try to protect it, the heart is vulnerable. That's why a grown man still feels like a little boy in his heart, and a mature woman still feels like a little girl inside.

So when we are working with a couple initially, we often use the terms little boy and little girl. Because little girls and little boys are safe. Children can just relax and have fun with each other.

When my Dad passed away, much of the family gathered in Vermont for His Memorial Service. Our son Jared is a pastor in West Virginia, and his church paid his expenses so he could come to participate in his grandfather's service. It was the first time Jared's children had been to Vermont. Our 4-year-old granddaughter met cousins that she hadn't met before. However, the cousins instantly got along great. They had fun playing together like they had known each other for years. That's what children can do, just relax and have fun together.

Often when we work with couples, they have experienced friction and, at times, even abuse in their relationship for years. In such cases, there is no way a wife is going to let her angry, verbally abusive husband anywhere near her heart, or a husband won't open his heart to his critical, controlling wife. However, if I can get the little boy to care about a frightened little girl, and the little girl to care about a hurting little boy; they will experience an emotionally connected relationship like nothing they have ever known. This is just an example.

I want you to understand what I mean by the terms "little boy" and "little girl".

❖ Remain sitting facing each other. Look into each other's eyes and relax for a couple of minutes.

Husband look at your wife's eyes and tell her…

(Wife's name), I am so glad God brought you into my life. From the beginning, I appreciated (the things you listed previously that attracted you to your wife). During our marriage, I have appreciated (the best part of your marriage).

I don't want to hurt or scare you. I want you to feel safe with me.

I want you to feel loved and cherished every day. Would you like that?

Allow your wife to answer.

Would it be ok if a little boy just cares about a little girl?

Allow your wife to answer.

Little boys and little girls can just relax together and enjoy being together. They can talk about anything. They have fun together. Would a little girl just like to have fun with a little boy?

Allow your wife to answer.

Can you tell me, how far is your heart from mine today?

Allow your wife to answer.

Is it all right if I keep working on it so our hearts grow even closer? Until they are connected as one?

Allow your wife to answer.

Can you tell me what the little girl is feeling right now?

Allow your wife to answer. Just care about whatever she shares. Don't argue or judge or lecture. Just care about what she shares.

Thank you for sharing that with me. I want to care about what you are feeling. You are important to me and your feelings are important to me. Is it ok if I pray for you?

If she says "Yes", you can use the following as a guide:

Jesus, I want to pray for (wife's name). I am so thankful that you brought us together. Thank You for giving me (wife's name). Please, help us both to be able to open our hearts to each other. Help us to grow closer emotionally. Jesus, my wife is feeling (what she just shared). Jesus, I know that You care about that. Please, help me to be more and more caring. Help me to love my wife in a way that she can feel my love every day. Jesus, please, speak to (wife's name)'s heart right now. Tell my wife how you feel about her. Please, show her how much You love her, Jesus.

Pause and allow Jesus to speak to your wife's heart. After a few minutes, ask if Jesus showed her anything. Then continue…

> *Jesus, thank You for loving us even more than we can imagine. I know that You have good things planned for our future. Help us both continue to grow closer to You and to each other. Amen.*

Now, it is the wife's turn. Look into your husband's eyes and tell him…

(Husband's name), I am glad that God brought you into my life. From the beginning, I appreciated (the things you listed previously that attracted you to your husband). During our marriage, I have appreciated (the best part of your marriage).

I don't want to hurt or control you. I want you to feel safe with me.

I want you to feel loved and respected every day. Would you like that?

Allow your husband to answer.

Is it all right if a little girl just cares about a little boy?

Allow your husband to answer.

Little girls aren't scary. They are safe. Would it be ok if the little girl and little boy just relax and have fun together?

Allow your husband to answer.

The little girl just wants to care about a little boy's heart. I want you to feel safe with me. I want you to be able to open your heart to me and share anything with me. Would you like that?

Allow your husband to answer.

On a scale of 1 to 100, how much do you feel loved by me today?

Allow your husband to answer.

Is it all right if I keep working on it, so I can get that up to 100%? I want you to feel loved and respected by me 100% every day. Would you like that?

Allow your husband to answer.

Thank you for sharing that with me. I want to care about what you are feeling. You are important to me and your feelings are important to me. Is it ok if I pray for you?

If he says "Yes", you can use the following as a guide:

Jesus, I want to pray for (husband's name). I am so thankful that you brought us together. Thank You for giving me (husband's name). Please, help us both to be able to open our hearts to each other. Help us to grow closer emotionally. Jesus. My husband is feeling (what he just shared). Jesus, I know that You care about that. Please, help me to be more and more caring. Help me to respect my husband in that so he can feel loved and respected. Jesus, please, speak to (husband's name)'s heart right now. Tell my husband how you feel about him. Please, show him how much You love him, Jesus.

Pause and allow Jesus to speak to your husband's heart. After a few minutes, ask if Jesus showed him anything. Then continue...

Jesus, thank You for loving us even more than we can imagine. I know that You have good things planned for our future. Help us both continue to grow closer to You and to each other.

Amen.

❖ Continue looking into each other's eyes. Take some time and talk about how you are both feeling now. Here are some questions you can ask each other:

- What was going on inside your heart, when I asked you those questions?
- Can you share with me what you are feeling right now?
- Can you tell me what your heart looks like right now?
- Would it be ok, if I cared about your heart every day for the rest of your life?
- Is it all right if I make you feel valued and accepted for the rest of your life?
- What can I say to make you feel valued and accepted?
- What can I do to make you feel valued and accepted?

Commitment to Continued Heart-Focused Communication

I hope that you thoroughly enjoyed this experience in heart-focused communication. Most couples do. Over the years, Wendy and I have led many couples to connect emotionally and communicate from the heart. However, no matter how well things go in our office, what makes the difference in relationships is what each couple does after they leave our office.

So I want to challenge you, commit to continue to "check in" and keep communicating with each other every day. Daily heart-focused communication goes beyond discussing the events of the day. It means communicating the feelings, both good and bad, that you each experienced that day. Wendy and I prioritize time every evening to share the struggles, feelings, and blessings we experienced that day. I want to challenge you to do the same. It is one of the best things you can do for your marriage and yourself.

❖ Here are some sample questions and statements you can use when you check in each day:

- Did you struggle with anything today? How did it make you feel? That must have been difficult, I just want you to know that I care that you felt that way.
- Did anything good happen today? How did it make you feel?
- Can you describe how your heart looks right now?
- Can a little boy/girl just care about a little girl/boy?

- ➤ I want you to feel safe to open your heart to me.
- ➤ I want you to be able to relax and feel safe with me.
- ➤ I just want to care about your heart.
- ➤ I don't want to control you. I won't criticize you.
- ➤ I want you to feel appreciated and respected by me.
- ➤ How can I pray for you right now? (Then stop and pray.)

I hope, after working through this chapter, you understand that heart-focused communication is much different than any other communication. It involves opening your heart to your spouse and sharing your deepest feelings and struggles with each other. It is communicating the deepest parts of being with your spouse and he (or she) opening to you. It is the kind of communication that we all long for, but few couples actually enjoy.

Wendy and I had been married 25 years before we learned to fully open our hearts and communicate on a heart level. We thought our relationship was good before because we had very little conflict. However, heart-focused communication and caring made our marriage better than we ever could have imagined. So I challenge you to commit to connecting with your spouse's heart every day. It is worth it!

In the next chapter, we will talk more about opening your heart to care about your spouse.

Review:

1. Think about a time when you and your spouse exchanged hurtful words.

    • How did your spouse's words hurt you?

    _____

    _____

    _____

    _____

- What did your words hurt your spouse?

_____

_____

_____

_____

- What was the outcome of that situation?

_____

_____

_____

_____

- How do you think God wanted you to resolve that situation?

_____

_____

_____

_____

2. Think about when you worked through this chapter and practiced heart-focused communication.

- How did you feel when your spouse looked in your eyes and asked your forgiveness for his/her hurtful words?

_____

_____

_____

_____

- How do you think he/she felt when you asked his/her forgiveness?

_____

_____

_____

_____

- How did you feel when your spouse looked in your eyes and asked heart-focused questions?

_____

_____

_____

_____

- How do you think your spouse felt when you did that?

_____

_____

_____

_____

- What do the two of you need to do to make sure that this heart-focused communication continues?

_____

_____

_____

_____

Prayer Time:

Theme Thought: I need to understand how my spouse and I have damaged each other with hurtful words. We need to forgive each other and commit to using our words to care about and encourage each other.

- Thank Jesus for helping you understand how you and your spouse have hurt each other with your words.
- Thank Jesus for helping you to forgive each other.
- Thank Jesus for helping you to open your hearts to each other.
- Thank Jesus for helping you to ask heart-focused questions.

- Thank Jesus for helping you to say caring, affirming statements to each other.
- Ask Jesus to help you to continue opening your heart to your spouse.
- Ask Jesus to help your spouse feel safe to open his/her heart to you.
- Ask Jesus to help you to say caring statements to your spouse every day.
- Ask Jesus to help you respond in a loving, caring way, regardless of what your spouse says.
- Ask Jesus to help you both to commit to heart-focused communication every day.
- Ask Jesus to show you every day how to demonstrate love and acceptance to your spouse.

11

THE CARING CYCLE

No one abuses his own body, does he? No, he feeds and pampers it. That's how Christ treats us, the church, since we are part of his body. And this is why a man leaves father and mother and cherishes his wife. No longer two, they become "one flesh." This is a huge mystery, and I don't pretend to understand it all. What is clearest to me is the way Christ treats the church. And this provides a good picture of how each husband is to treat his wife, loving himself in loving her, and how each wife is to honor her husband.

Ephesians 5: 29-33 *The Message*

In chapter 9, I talked about the Vicious Cycle. The good news is there is a better alternative. There is a better way of responding to each other. I call this the *Caring Cycle*. The Caring Cycle is simply the marriage relationship functioning the way God always intended. In the Caring Cycle the husband focuses on the wife and puts her needs before his own and the wife focuses on the husband and put his needs before her own. Most couples know they are supposed to do this, but don't know how to make it a reality in their respective marriages. In this chapter, I will walk you through the process and help you build a Caring Cycle in your marriage.

That being said, although God wants every couple to experience the Caring Cycle, the enemy, the world in which we live and our own sinful nature are opposed to each of us truly caring for our spouse at the deepest level. So what I am going to lead you to do will feel unnatural for many of you and may even make you uneasy at first.

In my younger days, I used to enjoy rappelling. If you don't know what that is, rappelling is descending rock faces and cliffs with ropes and a harness. The very first time I rappelled, I put on the harness, while my instructor fed the rope through a figure 8 descender and attached it to my harness with a locking carabiner. Then, the instructor had me stand at the edge of a cliff facing him and told me to lean back. I just stood there looking at him. The instructor, noticing my hesitation, said, "Trust the rope and your equipment. Lean back and you won't fall. If you don't lean back and you try descending, you will fall. This rope can hold 2000 pounds but it won't help you, if you don't trust it."

At his encouragement, I leaned back 90 degrees and began walking down the rock face. It was an awesome experience. About 20 feet down, there was an overhang, and I began descending vertically down the rope without my feet touching anything. I found that the instructor was right. Not only could I trust the rope completely, but by simply moving my braking hand a few inches I could slow my descent or even stop myself in midair. After that amazing experience, I would rappel every chance I had. I enjoyed finding even more challenging precipices to explore.

As much as I used to enjoy rappelling, I enjoy the Caring Cycle of my marriage much more. However, lowering my defenses and focusing on Wendy the first time, felt like standing at the edge of the cliff. It went against my natural responses and self-protective habits. I had to trust my wife and, even more, trust God. It was and continues to be the very best part of our marriage relationship.

The previous ten chapters have been preparing you for this chapter. All the work you have done has been to prepare you for this. You will have to trust me, the same way I had to trust that rope and my instructor. If you close this book now and walk away, I hope you will have benefited some; however, you won't experience the awesome caring relationship that God wants you to enjoy.

With harnesses on and ropes secure, lean back and follow me. The adventure awaits!

Identifying our Deepest Needs

Every week when we work with couples in our office, we do this same exercise with each couple. We instruct them to turn their chairs and face each other. We have them look into each other's eyes. Then, we lead them through the process of communicating on a heart level described in the last chapter. At the end of that time, I have the husband ask the wife, "What three things could I give you that would make you the happiest woman in the world?" I also lead the wife to ask her husband, "What three things could I give you that would make you the happiest man in the world?"

In answer to those questions, no person has ever asked for more money or a new car or a bigger house. Every person's answer always relates to their deepest emotional needs.

We all have two or three emotional needs. Usually, those emotional needs are the opposite of our emotional pain buttons described in chapter nine.

Here are some common emotional needs:

> ➤ To be accepted
> ➤ To be cherished
> ➤ To be affirmed
> ➤ To be appreciated for who I am
> ➤ To be respected
> ➤ To be understood
> ➤ To be listened to
> ➤ Time
> ➤ Affection

These are some of the most common emotional needs; however, this list is not exhaustive.

Take some quiet time now. Ask yourself this question, "What three things do I need to make me truly happy?" If you don't know how to answer this question, ask Jesus to reveal your greatest emotional needs.

List your answers in the following box.

My Three Greatest Emotional Needs:

1. _____
2. _____
3. _____

After leading a couple to define what each spouse needs emotionally, we have each person explain to the other how he (or she) can meet that need. For example, if a wife needs acceptance, I would have the husband ask his wife, "What can I do to help you feel accepted?" Or if a husband needs to be respected, I would have the wife ask her husband, "What can I do to help you feel accepted?"

Now, take some more quiet time and think about how your spouse could meet your three emotional needs. What actions or words would cause your needs to be met?

List your answers below.

My spouse can meet my needs by...

1) _____
   _____
2) _____
   _____
3) _____
   _____

Together Time: Sharing from the Heart

❖ Before we begin this next section, I'm going to ask you again to stop and pray together. Ask Jesus to help you both to be able to share from the heart. Again, I ask the husband to take the lead. Here is a prayer you can use if you wish.

Jesus, (__Wife's name__) and I want to be able to share openly and honestly. Would You help us both to feel safe? Help us both be able to open our hearts to each other. Remind us that You are here with us right now. Help us to accept what the other shares without reacting. Help us to open our heart to care about each other. Help us to understand what we each need to be fulfilled emotionally. Help us each to be willing to do all we can to meet the other's emotional needs.

Thank You, Jesus, that You are here with us and You will help us.

Amen.

❖ As a couple, sit looking into each other's eyes. Husband say to your wife...

(Wife's name), I am thankful that God has given you to me. I want to meet your deepest needs. What three things could I give you that would make you the happiest woman in the world?

Write your wife's answers on the following chart.

A. Wife's Three Greatest Emotional Needs:

1) _____
2) _____
3) _____

Husband continue asking...

(Wife's name), what can I do to meet these three emotional needs?

Write your wife's answers on the following chart.

Husband, ask your wife any clarifying questions so that you clearly understand what she needs and how you can meet those needs. Then, repeat what your wife has told you.

(Wife's name), you are saying that you need (#1 from box A) and I make you feel that when I (#1 from box B). You also need (#2 from box A), which you feel when I (#2 from box B). Then, you need (#3 from box A), which I can help you feel by (#3 from box B). I want to do my best so you feel (#1 from box A), (#2 from box A) and (#3 from box A) every day. Would you like that?

Allow your wife to answer.

❖ Now wife say to your husband...

(Husband's name), I am thankful that God has given you to me. I want to meet your deepest needs. What three things could I give you that would make you the happiest man in the world?

Write your husband's answers on the following chart.

Wife continue asking...

(Husband's name), what can I do to meet these three emotional needs?

Write your husband's answers on the following chart.

D. The wife can meet the husband's needs by...

1) _____

2) _____

3) _____

Wife, ask your husband any clarifying questions so that you clearly understand what she needs and how you can meet those needs. Then, repeat what your husband has told you.

(Husband's name), you are saying that you need (#1 from box A) and I make you feel that when I (#1 from box B). You also need (#2 from box A), which you feel when I (#2 from box B). Then you need (#3 from box A), which I can help you feel by (#3 from box B). I want to do my best so you feel (#1 from box A), (#2 from box A) and (#3 from box A) every day. Would you like that?

Allow your husband to answer.

Before continuing, pray for Jesus to help both of you meet the other's emotional needs. Here is a sample prayer you can use, if you wish.

Jesus, thank you for showing us our deepest emotional needs. Help us each to really understand what the other needs. Remind us every day to ask for Your help in meeting those needs. Help each of us to remember what the other needs and to commit to trying to meet those needs every day. Thank You that we don't have to do this on our own. You promise to help us.

Thank You, Jesus. Amen.

Identifying the Caring Cycle

In chapter 9, I helped you to identify the Vicious Cycle in your marriage. The good news is that you can replace your Vicious Cycle with the Caring Cycle. When your relationship experiences the Caring Cycle, both of you will have your emotional needs met. When the husband is meeting his wife's deepest emotional needs, she naturally wants to meet her husband's emotional needs. When the husband's deepest emotional needs are being met, he naturally wants to meet his wife's emotional needs. That is the Caring Cycle.

Now, let's identify the Caring Cycle for your marriage relationship. Fill in the following chart by referring back to boxes **A**, **B**, **C**, and **D**.

The Caring Cycle

B. (How Husband Meets Wife's Needs)

4. _____
5. _____
6. _____

HUSBAND

C. (Husband's Needs)   **A. (Wife's Needs)**

4. _____   1. _____
5. _____   2. _____
6. _____   3. _____

WIFE

D. (How Wife Meets Husband's Needs)

4. _____
5. _____
6. _____

You have now identified the Caring Cycle for your marriage. This is one of the most important exercises in this book. On this one chart, you have identified what you both need emotionally and how to meet each other's needs. I would encourage you to make several copies of this page in the book. Place the copies in places where you will see them often, so they are a constant reminder of what your spouse needs and how you can meet those needs. The more you fulfill your spouse emotionally, the more he or she will want to meet your needs. As long as the Caring Cycle is functioning in your relationship, the Vicious Cycle can't start spinning again. When both of your emotional needs are being met, neither of you will struggle emotionally nor respond out of pain.

Escaping the Vicious Cycle

I wish I could promise that as long as the two of you are caring for each other emotionally, you will never struggle with the Vicious Cycle again. However, that simply isn't true. We are still human and there are still times we all fall into old habits.

At times, Wendy and I still struggle with our own Vicious Cycle; however, much less than we used to do so. The good news is that there is a way to escape the Vicious Cycle and return to the Caring Cycle.

Refer back to chapter nine and review your Vicious Cycle. You will know that your spouse is struggling when you see that he or she is responding in his or her old pain response patterns (sections **B** and **D** in the chart). At that point, you have a decision to make. If you fall back into old pain response patterns, the Vicious Cycle will start spinning again. Instead, make the decision to show sacrificial love to your spouse by just caring for your spouse. In a very soft, gentle voice begin asking your spouse heart-focused questions to discover why he or she is struggling.

Here's an example:

(Spouse's name), you seem to be struggling. Did I do or say something to hurt you?

Allow your spouse to answer. If you did or said something, continue…

(Spouse's name), I'm sorry that I hurt you by (specific words or actions that hurt him or her). I was wrong, will you forgive me.

Sometimes, someone else or some event may be the cause. In which case say…

I'm sorry that happened to you. I just want you to know that I'm here for you. If you would like to talk about what happened, I would be glad to listen. Can I pray for you about that?

Then, pray for your spouse about the cause of his or her struggle. Ask Jesus to bring peace to his or her heart.

Sometimes, both spouses start struggling and fall back into their old patterns of responding to pain and hurting the other one. The Vicious Cycle begins whirling. The only way to stop that cycle is for one of the spouses to stop trying to protect himself or herself and begin caring about the other spouse. As soon as one of the spouses begins to care about the other, the Vicious Cycle will stop and the Caring Cycle will start again.

I will give you an example from our marriage. My wife, Wendy, and I have a regional counseling ministry. We work together most of the time. We counsel couples together. Some days, when we aren't counseling, we are in the office together working on various administrative responsibilities. When I am working, I become very task-focused. I can easily become so focused on what I am doing that I forget Wendy is even in the room. When that happens, Wendy feels alone, which is one of her pain buttons. She reacts by trying to control the situation so I pay attention to her. Then, I feel that I'm not living up to her expectations because failed expectations is one of my pain buttons. So then, I get more driven and work even harder, which makes her feel more alone. The Vicious Cycle is spinning again.

I can diffuse that situation by understanding that Wendy is responding with control because she is struggling emotionally. I know her well enough to know she is probably feeling alone. So I can stop what I'm doing, turn around and face Wendy and say calmly and gently,

"Wendy, I was so busy, I made you feel alone, didn't I? I'm sorry I did that. You are more important to me than any of my work. I don't want you to feel lonely. I want you to feel loved and accepted by me all the time. Will you forgive me for hurting you?"

The Vicious Cycle will not continue if you just begin showing genuine care and concern for your spouse. Unselfish caring will always stop that cycle.

Sometimes, when the Vicious Cycle gets spinning, neither one of you knows what to say, stop and pray. Ask Jesus to help you. Ask Him to give you the right words to say to each other. Ask Him to help you show genuine love to each other. Jesus will always answer those prayers. He loves to help us if we will simply ask for His help.

> If any of you lacks wisdom, let him ask of God, who gives to all liberally and without reproach, and it will be given to him. (James 1:5)

This is one of my favorite verses. In marriage, as in many other areas of life, there are times I don't know what to say or do. When I humble myself and ask for God's wisdom, He always answers. When a couple recognizes they need God's help and cry out to Him, He loves to respond by giving them the wisdom they need for that situation. God always keeps His promises.

The Caring Cycle is the key to the emotionally connected relationship that God wants every couple to enjoy. Now that you have identified your Caring Cycle, as a couple, commit to meeting each other's emotional needs every day. You will never regret this commitment.

Review:

1. In this chapter, did you learn anything about yourself that you didn't understand before? _____ If so, what?

_____

_____

_____

_____

2. Did you learn anything about your spouse that you didn't understand before? _____ If so, what?

_____

_____

_____

_____

3. How did you feel when your spouse asked you about your three emotional needs?

_____

_____

_____

_____

4. How do you think you will feel when your spouse meets your three needs every day?

_____

_____

_____

_____

5. How do you think your spouse will feel when you meet his/her three needs every day?

_____

_____

_____

_____

Prayer Time:

Theme Thought: I need to understand my emotional needs, as well as my spouse's emotional needs. I need to commit to meeting my spouse's needs every day. I need to care about my spouse when we get caught in the Vicious Cycle.

- Thank Jesus for helping you understand what you need emotionally.
- Thank Jesus for helping you to understand what your spouse needs emotionally.
- Ask Jesus to help you both to continue to grow in your understanding of each other's needs.
- Ask Jesus to help you meet your spouse's emotional needs every day.
- Ask Jesus to remind you of the ways you can meet your spouse's needs every day.
- Ask Jesus to help you to put your spouse's needs before your own.
- Ask Jesus to help you be able to humble yourself and care about your spouse when he/she is struggling.
- Ask Jesus to help you both to be able to stop the Vicious Cycle.

12

MOVING FORWARD

Summing up: Be agreeable, be sympathetic, be loving, be compassionate, be humble. That goes for all of you, no exceptions. No retaliation. No sharp-tongued sarcasm. Instead, bless—that's your job, to bless. You'll be a blessing and also get a blessing.

I Peter 3:8, 9 *The Message*

You made it! This is the final chapter.

I remember hiking with Wendy in the White Mountains of New Hampshire. No matter how difficult the climb, standing on the summit always brought feelings of exhilaration. The pain and exhaustion of the climb were forgotten.

You have almost finished this book; however, the adventure of enjoying an emotionally connected marriage relationship is just beginning. This book is just the trailhead for your journey. In this chapter, I want to give you some important tools to help you enjoy and succeed in a lifetime of connecting with and caring for your spouse.

Relational Projects

At the end of a week of intensive counseling with a couple, we give them things to work on at home to keep growing in their relationship. We used to call these assignments "homework." However, we worked with several men who hated school. When we told them they had homework, their eyes fogged over and they checked out mentally.

So, we now call these assignments, "relational projects". Most men like doing projects. Whatever you want to call them, these are important tools that will help you continue to grow closer in your relationship. These relational projects will reinforce everything that you read and worked through as you went through this book.

It took commitment for you, not just to read this book, but to also answer the questions and do the assignments. I want to challenge you to also commit to doing these projects. If you wait to do them until you feel like doing them, you never will. Your marriage is worth it! Commit to following through and doing these projects. You won't regret it and neither will your spouse.

A couple in their eighties recently called and scheduled to come for a week of counseling. They have been married for 58 years. The wife told me they have a good relationship, but they want to learn some things that can help them have an even closer relationship. I was impressed. We all need that commitment and willingness to do whatever we can to keep growing closer to our spouse. I hope I never stop growing closer to Wendy. I hope the same for you and your spouse.

Project 1: Pray Together

The first assignment that we give every couple is simply to pray together every day. You would be surprised how few Christian couples pray together. Many wives desperately want their husbands to pray with them; however, most husbands struggle with doing that. There are a number of different reasons why husbands are reticent to pray with their wives. However, I believe that the main reason couples don't pray together is that the enemy hates it when couples pray together. So, he will do all he can to stop it from happening.

Jesus promised, "For where two or three are gathered together in My name, I am there in the midst of them." When a husband and wife pray together God moves in powerful ways.

Jesus didn't say, "Where fifty or one hundred are gathered together in my name." He said that when only two are gathered together in His name, He is right there with them. This means whenever a husband and wife join together in prayer, Jesus is right there with them.

Years ago, a pastor friend encouraged me to pray with Wendy every day. That was some of the best advice we ever received. We have experienced Jesus' presence in amazing ways. We have seen God answer our prayers in truly miraculous ways.

So, your first assignment is to prioritize time to pray together every day. Don't wait until you both feel like praying. It won't happen. Plan time into your schedule every day when you can pray together. It doesn't have to be a long period of time. It can be only five or ten minutes a day, but praying together has to be a priority. Make a concerted effort to pray together every day until it becomes a habit. Even then, guard your time. Don't allow the tyranny of the urgent to steal your prayer time.

This prayer time is not a time when you pray for your family, your friends, your church and the missionaries. Those things are important and you should pray for them. However, this prayer time is when you pray for your relationship. Husband, pray for your wife and any struggles she may be having. Wife, pray for your husband and any struggles he may be having. Ask God to protect your relationship. Ask Him to help you stay emotionally connected. Thank God for His blessings and answers to prayer.

Praying together as a couple is one of the best things you can do for your relationship. You will be amazed at how your hearts will be welded together as you pray with and for each other. You will experience God answering your prayers in incredible ways.

Project 2: Connect Emotionally

In chapter 10, I walked you through the process of connecting emotionally using heart-focused questions. It is important that you continue connecting emotionally every day. This does not have to take a lot of time; however, at least ten minutes every day you need to spend time "checking in" with each other emotionally.

You can connect emotionally by...

1. Focusing on each other's eyes.
2. Holding hands.
3. Talking totally focused on each other.
4. Using affirming touch, such as a hug or arm around your spouse's shoulder.
5. Asking heart-focused questions

Your purpose during this time is to focus on your spouse's heart, not his or her body. There is nothing wrong with a married couple desiring each other sexually. Sex was designed by God as a special part of the marriage relationship. However, during the time you are connecting emotionally each of you needs to focus on the other person's heart and emotions.

Many couples only know how to connect sexually and not emotionally. Many times, the wife comes away from sex feeling used and unfulfilled. So, it is important during this time to focus on caring emotionally about the other person. When a husband is caring for his wife emotionally, she will gladly give herself physically to him. However, that is not the purpose of this time. This time is simply to focus on building an emotional connection. When you are emotionally connected, your sex life will be better than ever.

It is important that during this time, you both can share any struggles with each other. Share how you felt about them. This is the one time every day when each of you can share anything with the one person who loves you more than anyone else. As you listen to your spouse, simply care about what he or she is saying. You don't have to "fix" anything, just care about what he or she shares.

For example, my Wendy often counsels women by herself. If a woman is more dominant than her or is angry and doesn't listen to her, that person very well could step on Wendy's pain buttons. So, when we are connecting, if Wendy shares that she struggled with that person, I just care about what she is sharing. I don't have to confront that person. I just have to show Wendy that I care. I do that by saying something like, "I'm sorry she did that to you. That wasn't right. I just want you to know that I care and I'm here for you."

Asking heart-focused questions is an important part of connecting emotionally. I gave you a list of such questions in chapter ten.

❖ Here are some more heart-focused questions you can use:

➤ What have you enjoyed the most about our years together?

➤ What is your favorite thing for us to do together?

➤ If we could go anywhere in the world together, where would you like to go? Why?

➤ What is your biggest fear? Why do you think that is?

➤ Do you ever get discouraged? What things cause you to be discouraged?

➤ Do you feel affirmed by me? If so, what do I do to make you feel affirmed? If not, what could I do to make you feel affirmed?

➤ Do you feel valued by me? If so, what do I do that makes you feel valued? If not, what can I do to make you feel valued?

➤ Do you ever feel that I try to control you? If so when? How does it make you feel?

➤ Do you usually feel that I'm sensitive to your needs? How does it make you feel if I'm insensitive?

➤ How can I better meet your emotional needs?

➤ Do you ever feel lonely? If so when? How can I keep you from feeling lonely?

➤ How would you feel if I cared about your heart every day for the rest of our lives?

These two lists of questions are simply tools you can use to help you to build an emotional connection in your relationship. As the two of you become more comfortable talking about and sharing your emotions, you can come up with your own questions. Every couple is different, so you need to work together to find what works best for the two of you.

Make sure that you plan and prioritize time every day when you can emotionally connect. Do whatever you have to do to plan this time in your schedule. Husbands and wives both need this emotional connection. It's important!

Project 3: Make Decisions Together

In most marriages, one spouse is usually more dominant than other. So often, the dominant spouse makes all the decisions. Occasionally, both spouses are dominant and they both want to make all the decisions. Then sometimes, couples are like Wendy and me, where neither spouse is dominant and neither one wants to make the decisions.

Regardless of your natural bent as a leader or a follower, it is important that in your marriage you make decisions together. God did establish the husband to be the Christ-like servant leader in marriage. However, God never meant for the husband to be a dictator who makes all the decisions. The husband and wife are to work together with God's help to make decisions.

Many couples struggle, with making decisions together. So, I will give you a simple outline to walk you through the decision-making process.

1. *Define the Decision.* What is the decision you need to make? The husband shares how he sees the decision. The wife shares how she sees the decision. Husbands and wives view things differently. Talk about the decision, so you both understand the other's point of view. The purpose of this part of the process is clarification and understanding, not debate, so just accept your spouse's point of view.
2. *Discuss Potential Outcomes.* Discuss all the possibilities. You might what to actually write down all the possible decisions that you could make. Brainstorm and list all your ideas.
3. *Pray for God's Direction.* You pray about this decision until God shows both of you what He wants. Obviously, God's way is always best. So, you need His direction to know the right decision. God will never tell the husband one thing and the wife another. So, you continue to pray until God confirms to both of you what He wants you to do. God will never tell the husband one thing and the wife another. He will confirm to both of you what decision He wants you to make. This third step is the most important. Pray and allow God to guide your decisions.

Project 4: Stop the Vicious Cycle

As I said in the last chapter, there will be times when you fall back into your old Vicious Cycle. So, don't be shocked when it happens. It just proves that you and your spouse still have your human natures. The key is not staying in that cycle. I explained in the last chapter how to get out of the Vicious Cycle and back to the Caring Cycle.

I just want to add a word of caution. We encourage couples not to use the words *never, always* or *but*. Often when the Vicious Cycle starts spinning, it is easy to begin using hurtful comments or invalidating statements. For example:

"You *always* do this."

"You *never* listen to me."

These are unfair exaggerations which attack our spouse's character. Using the words "never" or "always" during a disagreement is always damaging and never a good idea.

Also, don't use the word but when you are having a disagreement. For example:

"I understand that you are upset, *but* you are overreacting."

When you use the word "but" in a statement, you cancel out whatever you said before the "but." In the example statement, if I had stopped with the first six words, it would have been a good, caring statement. It would have demonstrated that I realize the other person is upset and I care about that. However, by adding the "but" and the for words that follow, I invalidate the person's feelings. Rather than the other person feeling cared for, they end up feeling put down and judged.

When you find yourself in the Vicious Cycle again, resist the urge to use the words *never, always,* and *but*. Instead, begin making caring statements to your spouse. Also, remember to stop and pray together for God to help you escape the Vicious Cycle and return to the Caring Cycle. When a couple humbles themselves and asks God's help, He always answers. God will gladly help you to humbly care for your spouse and vice versa. He loves it when His people cast their cares and anxieties on Him and experience Him caring for them. (I Pet. 5:7)

Project 5: Do Random Acts of Kindness

A number of years ago Wendy and I taught in Christian School. Since we only taught during the school year, we didn't work during the summer. When our children became teenagers, we decided as a family to use our summers to serve the Lord in a ministry. So, for five summers, the four of us served at Victory Bible Camp in Alaska. Our son, Jared, and daughter, Melanie, worked with us the first year. After that, they served as assistant counselors and eventually counselors. One summer, the counseling staff did a fun activity. Each week, they would draw names of another counselor or assistant counselor. Then that week, they would look for opportunities to secretly do what they called "random acts of kindness" for that person. Wendy worked in the camp gift shop, so counselors would come to her to find out what kind of snacks their person-of-the-week preferred. This activity was enjoyable for those involved, as well as those of us who were simply observers.

Wendy and I borrowed this idea. We now encourage couples to look for opportunities to do random acts of kindness for each other. This doesn't have to cost anything. It can be as simple as a note in your spouse's lunch box. Or a daisy you picked alongside the road. Or a foot rub or back rub after a long day. The possibilities are endless.

Look for opportunities to do something for your spouse just to let him or her know that you love him or her and are thinking of him or her. You could stop on the way home from work and pick up flowers or your spouse's favorite hot beverage. However, these simple acts don't have to cost money. Usually, the most meaningful acts of kindness don't cost anything but time.

Husbands especially are quicker to buy flowers or candy for their wives than take the time to write a short love note or a simple poem. However, the simple acts that take more of our time and thought usually mean more to our wives. Men, your wife knows you better than anyone. She knows when you do something for her that really took effort and time. She also knows when you just buy something without really putting thought into it. So, challenge yourself a little. Try writing a poem or a song. Make an acrostic with your wife's name and with each letter tell something you appreciate about her. These things will mean a lot to your wife even though they may not be perfect.

So, we encourage each husband and wife to actively look for opportunities to do little things to let your spouse know you are thinking of him or her. Doing random acts of kindness will be enjoyable for both the doer and the receiver. These simple actions help to keep the Caring Cycle going and the Vicious Cycle from starting again.

Project 6: Share One Blessing Every day

I also want to encourage you to look for at least one blessing every day. Then share that blessing with your spouse. Wendy and I share our blessings every evening as part of our connecting time.

In chapter four, I shared how God convicted me of my negative attitude. I also shared that Wendy and I record and share our blessings every day. Looking for blessings each day really changed my focus and my attitude. It has been a very good thing for my relationship with God and my wife. Wendy and I really enjoy sharing our blessings. Some days, it is just a blessing to make it through the day. Other days, we see God move in miraculous ways and it is exciting to share those things together.

Several years ago, we were counseling a very difficult couple. They had a lot of tension and conflict in their relationship. The first day in our office, they refused to look at or talk to each other. We could feel the tension in the room. That evening, I asked Wendy if she had any blessings that day. With a sigh, she answered, "Nobody hit anybody today!"

God's blessings fill our days. Sometimes, He blesses us in magnanimous, miraculous ways, but often His blessings come in small ways throughout our days. When you look for God's blessings, you will begin to realize how blessed you really are. Sharing blessings together helps a couple to grow closer to God and each other, as they grow in gratitude together.

Project 7: Plan for Accountability

The couples that do best after counseling are those that have a system of accountability. No matter how well the week of counseling goes, what matters, in the long run, is whether or not the couple is continuing to do these relational projects. It really helps to have accountability partners or an accountability group that holds the couple responsible to follow through.

When a couple gets back home, it is very easy to get lazy and fall back into old habits. Sometimes, we encourage every couple to find a mature Christian couple in their church or community that they trust. Together pray about this and decide who that couple should be. Choose a couple that won't be soft on you but will challenge you and pray for you. Then, ask them if they would meet with you the two of you regularly, preferably at least once a month.

Unfortunately, many couples don't know a mature couple that meets these criteria. In that case, the husband should choose a godly man and the wife should choose a godly woman to be their respective accountability partners. Both the husband and wife should meet with their accountability partners regularly. Again, the accountability partner should be someone who cares enough about you to confront when you fail but also encourages you to do better. It should be someone you can trust to pray for you but keep everything shared completely confidential. This is not a time to complain about your spouse. This is a time to share how you are doing on following through with your part of the relational projects.

I know of a few churches that have encouragement/accountability groups for those couples that have been through counseling. These couples get together regularly, usually once or twice a month. Each couple shares how they are doing. When a couple is struggling, the group prays for and encourages them. When a couple is doing well, the group celebrates together. Again, this is not a venue for a disgruntled person to vent about his or her spouse. The group leaders need to make sure that doesn't happen. Everything shared in the group must be held in strict confidentiality by everyone in the group. It would be a good idea for each person to sign a confidentiality agreement when they join the group. An example of a Confidentiality Statement is on the next page. You can adapt this statement to your needs.

I only know of a few churches that have these accountability and support groups for their people. I really wish there were more. Maybe you should pray and ask God if He wants you to help start such a group in your own church. One of the reasons I wrote this book was so that churches can use it in a small group setting to help couples. Ideally, a group of couples would work through this book together. Each couple would do their own work at home of course, but then when the group meets they could discuss that week's subject together. Ideally, after finishing the book, the group will continue to meet in order to hold each other accountable and encourage long-term follow through. If you are studying this book as a group, pray about continuing to meet in order to facilitate this very important accountability.

STATEMENT OF CONFIDENTIALITY

I understand that everything discussed in the Marriage Encouragement Group is totally confidential. I understand that the discussion in these sessions must be held in the strictest confidence. Under no circumstances, may information pertaining to anyone in the group be discussed outside the group sessions.

I understand that failure to abide by this Statement of Confidentiality may cause my removal from this group. I have read this statement and agree to comply with these restrictions.

Signature _____ Date _____

Printed Name _____

Address _____

City/State/Postal Code _____

Phone _____ Email _____

If you don't belong to an accountability group, let me encourage you to find that mature, godly couple or individual that can help you in this way. Do this right away, as soon as you finish this book. Don't put it off. Don't wait until you have more time. It will never happen if you don't make this a priority. Talk to your spouse about this. Pray about it together. Work through the "decision-making process" to decide together who God wants to be your accountability partner. God already knows you the right couple or individuals are. Allow Him to guide you in this process. Accountability partners are an important investment in the future of your marriage.

Now, you may be wondering, "How does my accountability person know what to ask?" On the next page, there is an Accountability Guide for you and your spouse to complete together. Then, you both sign it at the bottom and photocopy that page of this book. You may then give the copy to your accountability partner(s) as a guideline for them to use when you have your accountability meetings. It also should prompt them to pray for you in these areas.

As I close, I want to encourage you once again to commit to actually doing these seven relational projects. Taking the time to read and work through this book was important, but it is only the first step. Following through is what will benefit your marriage relationship next week, next month, next year and for years to come. It will take time and commitment to do these projects. If you just wait until you feel like doing them, they won't happen. As you do these faithfully, they will become habitual. You and your spouse will both benefit. You will both enjoy an emotionally connected marriage as God designed. It doesn't get any better than that!

Photocopy of the Accountability Guide on this page is permitted only for accountability purposes.

Accountability Guide

Two are better than one…A cord of three strands is not quickly broken. Eccl. 4:9,12 NIV

We as a couple have committed to doing the following things for the good of our marriage. We request that you pray for us and hold us accountable in these areas.

1. Praying together every day.
2. Spending time connecting emotionally every day.
3. Seeking God's direction for decisions and making those decisions together.
4. Stopping the Vicious Cycle. When we have conflict, we will each do our part to care about the other person and return to the Caring Cycle.
5. Each seeks opportunities to do random acts of kindness for the other person.
6. Share at least one blessing every day.
7. We are willing to be held accountable in these areas. We agree to meet regularly with our accountability partner(s).
8. Prayer needs:

❖ The greatest struggle in our marriage has been…

_____

_____

❖ The greatest victory in our marriage has been…

_____

_____

❖ Our greatest prayer needs are…

_____

_____

By signing this, we agree to allow this person(s) to hold us accountable.
Husband's signature: _____
Wife's signature: _____
By signing this we agree to meet regularly and hold the above signed person(s) accountable.
Accountability Partner's signature: _____
Accountability Partner's signature: _____

Review:

1. Before reading this book how often did you and your spouse pray together? _____ How do you think praying together every day could benefit your marriage relationship?

    _____

    _____

    _____

    _____

2. As you read through this book, you had opportunities to emotionally connect with your spouse. Did you enjoy those opportunities? _____ Do you think that your spouse enjoyed them? _____

    - How do you think you would feel, if your spouse cared about you and connected emotionally with you every day for the rest of your lives?

    _____

    _____

    _____

    _____

    - How do you think your spouse would feel?

    _____

    _____

    _____

    _____

3. In the past, who usually made most of the decisions in your marriage? _____

   - How do you think making decisions together could help your relationship?

   _____

   _____

   _____

   _____

   - How would allowing God to guide your decisions affect your marriage?

   _____

   _____

   _____

   _____

4. If the Vicious Cycle starts to spin, what could you do to care about your spouse and help start the Caring Cycle again?

   _____

   _____

   _____

   _____

5. What are some random acts of kindness you could do for your spouse this week?

_____

_____

_____

_____

6. What is one way God has blessed you today?

_____

_____

_____

_____

How has God blessed you this week?

_____

_____

_____

_____

How has He blessed you this month?

_____

_____

_____

_____

7. List possible accountability partners:

_____   _____

_____   _____

_____   _____

_____   _____

Prayer Time:

Theme Thought: I need to commit on doing my part to continuously make my marriage better. I understand that follow through is an important part of growing closer to my spouse. I know that I need God's help to do this. I also need a person I trust who will hold me accountable.

- Thank Jesus for helping you to finish this book.
- Thank Jesus for helping you to understand yourself better.
- Thank Jesus for helping you to understand your spouse better.
- Ask Jesus to help you both to continue to grow in your understanding of each other.

- Ask Jesus to help both of you to prioritize time talking to Him together every day.
- Ask Jesus to help you to prioritize a time to connect emotionally every day.
- Ask Jesus to help you make decisions together with His guidance.
- Ask Jesus to help you stop the vicious cycle and care for each other any time that you struggle.
- Ask Jesus to help you look for opportunities to do nice things for your spouse.
- Ask Jesus to help you see His blessings every day.
- Ask Jesus for wisdom in finding the right accountability partners.
- Ask Jesus to help you be faithful in following through with all you have learned in this book.

In closing, I want to thank you for caring enough about your marriage to actually finish this book. I want you to know that I prayed for you as I wrote this book, I prayed for you as it was being published and I would like to pray for you now.

Jesus, thank you for each husband and wife who read this book. Thank you for each engaged couple that read this book. I thank you for their commitment. Jesus, you know that some of the areas discussed in this book were not easy to deal with. Some of the exercises were not easy to complete. I thank You, Jesus, for helping each one to finish this book. I ask You to help each couple continue connecting with one another. Enable them to stop the Vicious Cycle when it begins to spin. Help each husband to love his wife sacrificially and truly care for her. Help the husband to be the spiritual leader of his home. Help each wife to lovingly and respectfully follow her husband's lead. Help each couple to continue growing in their relationship with You and with each other. Thank You, Jesus, that you have good things planned for their future as they allow You the central place in their marriage. I commit each person who read this book to You today, Jesus. Accomplish Your wonderful will in his or her life and marriage.

In Your glorious name, Amen.

If we can assist you in any way, please, contact *Caring for the Heart – New England* (www.cfth-ne.org). May God bless you as you build a connected relationship and enjoy the amazing adventure that is marriage!

Bibliography

Sacred Marriage was written by Gary Thomas and published in 2015 by Zondervan.

Scripture quotes were taken from the following translations:

- **New King James Version®**. Copyright © 1982 by Thomas Nelson. Used by permission. All rights reserved.
- **NEW AMERICAN STANDARD BIBLE®**, Copyright © 1960,1962,1963,1968,1971,1972,1973,1975,1977,1995 by The Lockman Foundation. Used by permission.
- *The Message* was written by Eugene Peterson. Copyright © 1993, 1994, 1995, 1996, 2000, 2001, 2002. Used by permission of NavPress Publishing Group.
- *Holy Bible*, **New Living Translation**, copyright © 1996, 2004, 2015 by Tyndale House Foundation. Used by permission of Tyndale House Publishers, Inc., Carol Stream, Illinois 60188. All rights reserved.

Printed in the United States
By Bookmasters